Cottage Garden Flowers

RHS WISLEY HANDBOOKS

Cottage Garden Flowers

Sue Phillips

MITCHELL BEAZLEY

THE ROYAL HORTICULTURAL SOCIETY

Cottage Garden Flowers
Sue Phillips

First published in Great Britain in 2003 by Cassell Illustrated, an imprint
of Octopus Publishing Group Limited.
This edition published in 2008 in association with the Royal
Horticultural Society by Mitchell Beazley, an imprint of Octopus
Publishing Group Limited, 2–4 Heron Quays, London E14 4JP
An Hachette Livre UK Company
www.octopusbooks.co.uk

ISBN 978 1 84533 375 1

Commissioning Editor Camilla Stoddart
Designer Justin Hunt

Set in Bembo

Colour reproduction by Dot Gradations Ltd.
Printed and bound by Toppan in China

CONTENTS

Previous page:
A typical old-
fashioned cottage
garden is a complete
jumble of flowers just
enjoying themselves.

Introduction

Cottage garden flowers are evocative of the romance, unhurried pace of life and down-to-earth practicality of small, self-sufficient gardens of a bygone age. The stars of chocolate boxes and Victorian watercolours, they are natural survivors that have outlasted the whims of fashion and continue to appeal to today's plant lovers, who appreciate them for the same characteristics for which old cottagers grew them – their bravery, reliability and determination.

There is no formal definition of cottage garden flowers, and they cover an enormous range of families and genera. Most are hardy, and they include a mixture of British native wildflowers and their close relatives, herbs with a wide range of culinary and household uses, bee plants, and a huge number of traditional hardy annual and perennial flowers that have old-fashioned character, even if they are not always truly old varieties. They are sociable flowers that naturally go well together, and look at home in the rambling, overcrowded beds and borders that are typical of traditional cottage gardens.

While some cottage garden flowers are real treasures – highly collectable 'living antiques' that need special care – the bulk of them are very forgiving, easy-going plants that were originally grown by poor country people who had neither the time, the space or the money to go in for anything other than the most basic, self-sufficient form of gardening. Cottage garden flowers are undemanding and easy to propagate; they had to be, otherwise they would not have survived.

Today, cottage garden flowers are perfect for gardeners who

The term 'cottage garden flowers' covers a huge range of species grown in orderly chaos.

enjoy 'pottering'. They are ideal for busy people, or those who want a 'proper' garden that they can enjoy without making a lot of heavy work for themselves. They suit horticultural renegades who want to garden in their own way, without slavishly sticking to rules or following a tight gardening schedule. They appeal particularly to those who like a very informal, flowery look and who need a style of gardening that allows them to pack as much as possible into a limited space.

However, cottage garden flowers do not have to be grown traditionally – the plants are very adaptable and suit the new natural look, as well as flowering meadow and 'prairie' styles of planting. Their ranks have also been joined by newer varieties of old favourites and flowers that, strictly speaking, are not traditional cottage garden types but just happen to suit the orderly chaos of the typically crowded cottage garden planting style.

The one thing you can safely say about cottage garden flowers is that you do not need a quaint old country cottage in order to grow them – they can look equally at home around a bungalow, town house or even in containers on the balcony of a flat, as long as their surroundings are reasonably traditional.

Overcrowded, old-fashioned flowers and traditional features, such as sundials or birdbaths, are hallmarks of cottage gardens.

WHAT ARE COTTAGE GARDEN FLOWERS?

Plants grown for their good looks alone were a luxury that hardworking people could ill afford, so the original cottage garden flowers were useful as well as ornamental. They provided nectar for the cottagers' bees – particularly early in the spring, before the fruit trees came into bloom or there were many flowers out in the fields and countryside – and the raw materials for a huge range of medicines, toiletries, dyes and other household goods, all of which early cottagers had to make for themselves.

Since livestock and productive plants like vegetables and fruit were the mainstay of an early cottage garden, flowers would be confined to the front garden or a small patch on either side of the path. They also had to be capable of fending for themselves, as farm labourers did not have the time to indulge in gardening as a hobby, so the only flowers that survived were the more aggressively spreading perennials and self-seeding hardy annuals.

As affluence increased and a greater range of plants became available, cottagers also grew flowers such as dahlias, sweet peas and gladioli in rows in their vegetable gardens, to cut and sell at the garden gate for pin-money. However, since cottagers did not own greenhouses, it was not until comparatively recent times that frost-tender plants like nicotianas and pelargoniums joined the ranks of 'traditional' cottage garden flowers.

Modern gardeners, with a far wider range of plants at their disposal, will also add plants that are not authentic cottage garden flowers, for extra interest or in order to 'stretch' the traditional spring and summer flowering season into autumn and winter.

Cottage gardens are meant to look as if they 'happened' all by themselves, so drifts of wildflowers, self-seeding annuals and spreading perennials add to the illusion.

Cottage garden flowers through history

History devotes a lot of coverage to the landed gentry, whose stately homes and country houses were surrounded by important gardens created as elaborate status symbols. They were deliberately designed, stocked with rare, expensive and often newly introduced plants, and carefully maintained by a large staff of highly trained craftsmen. They contained a wealth of architectural features, walled kitchen gardens complete with greenhouses for out-of-season produce, and leisure facilities such as walks and croquet lawns, and they have been preserved, restored and improved by a succession of owners over the centuries, so it is relatively easy to follow their history.

In contrast, little is heard of the tenants of the gentry: the small-scale farmers, artisans and peasants who worked on the land and lived in hovels, and whose gardens were purely for self-sufficiency, but it is from these groups that cottage garden plants originate. It is very difficult to separate cottage flowers from the gardens in which they grew and the people who grew them – their roots are firmly embedded in social history.

The very earliest cottage gardens of the 14th century were more like primitive smallholdings, where people grew fodder for domestic livestock and a few fruit trees and vegetables. The first 'flowers' would have been herbs, which were used all around the house, not just in the kitchen. Cottagers worked long hours and had large families to support, and they relied on their garden to provide a lot of life's essentials. The family would keep bees and a selection of livestock, and they grew herbs for a variety of household uses, but along the way they acquired a few purely ornamental flowers to grow in small areas at the front of the cottage or alongside a path.

These flowers were either sports of common wildflowers, which stood out due to their double flowers or unusual colouring, or they were hand-me-downs from the great gardens of the wealthy, where the cottagers' sons worked as trainee gardeners. Since cottagers did not have money to spare for plants, cottage garden flowers were not bought and sold but were passed around freely among families, friends and neighbours. The plants that became cottage garden favourites

The rustic 'home-made' cottage-look is now the height of fashion as 'natural' gardening.

were those that survived a high degree of neglect, had a strong instinct for survival in overcrowded conditions, and were easily propagated by saving their seed or by 'breaking bits off and sticking them in'.

Industrial progress led to many workers leaving the land and moving to the towns, taking some of their plants with them to make small artisans' gardens. Rising prosperity brought about a middle class, who also grew and bred 'florists' flowers' as a hobby and competed for prizes at 'florists' feasts', which were the first flower shows. Florists' flowers are unlikely to have been grown by true country cottagers, as they would have been time-consuming and expensive; however, just like topiary, potagers and knot gardens, over time they have been 'borrowed' from wealthier gardens and nowadays often come under the modern-day cottage gardener's wing.

Despite the various upturns and downturns in economic conditions, life did not change very much for cottagers who remained on the land. They still lived in pretty dreadful conditions even by Victorian times, when romantic depictions of ramshackle cottages and semi-wild gardens, with hollyhocks at the gate and roses around the door, prompted the trend for the newly rich professional classes to take over old cottages and turn them into weekend retreats. The influx of new wealth meant that cottagers now had a market for cut flowers and fresh produce, as well as new neighbours with whom to swap plants, all of which went some way towards enriching the living standards of the rural under-class.

Unlike the gardens of the rich, cottage gardens were never planned – they 'just happened'. New additions were simply shoe-horned in anywhere there was room, which led to the characteristically charming, higgledy-piggledy style. Gardening fashions of the rich have come and gone over the centuries, but the gardens of the poor have changed very little – which is why so many old cottage flowers have survived. In recent times, a great many of them have been rediscovered in old cottage gardens in Ireland and the West Country. In the prosperous regions, gardeners had the money to redesign and restock in order to keep up to date with formal bedding gardens, low-maintenance groundcover gardens and so forth, which meant that a lot of old-fashioned flowers were lost as nurseries no longer found it worthwhile to keep stocks. Fortunately, flower gardening came back into fashion, however, and now a lot of once hard-to-find plants are back in favour.

The great beauty of having a cottage garden nowadays is that all sorts of plants can be incorporated into it without looking out of place. This makes it a good garden style for the compulsive plant enthusiast who cannot stop buying interesting things at nurseries, plant fairs and shows, and who wants to grow a bit of everything while still having a garden that 'hangs together'. Even so, for it to look like a cottage garden the core plants are the traditional old-fashioned types.

The naming of cottage garden flowers

For some people, part of the charm of old cottage garden flowers lies in their endearing Olde Worlde common names, such as fox-and-cubs – an orange-flowered hawkweed (*Pilosella aurantiaca*), or cherubim and seraphim – a very early flowering comfrey (*Symphytum grandiflorum*). Some of the common names derive from the appearance of the flower – fox-and-cubs has heads of fox red, furry flowers – or the place where it grew, such as wallflower (*Erysimum cheiri*). Many plants used for medicinal purposes were named according to the Doctrine of Signatures, an ancient belief that the Almighty stamped certain plants with a sign to indicate their use. For example, lungwort (*Pulmonaria officinalis*), which has spotty leaves, was supposed to cure lung diseases, and viper's bugloss (*Echium vulgare*), with scaly stems and dead flowerheads the same shape as a snake's head, was reputed to cure snake bite.

The problem is that a lot of common flower names are very

Traditionally, flowers were grown in the front garden and vegetables at the back of the house. Now we tend to put flowers everywhere with only a small vegetable patch, if any.

localised and vary around the country, so that one plant may have a number of different common names, often making it difficult to pinpoint precisely the plant involved. The old names may have a great appeal, but for accuracy it is a good idea to link them with the Latin name, which itself can tell you something about the uses of particular kinds of plants. Some herbs, for instance, were thought to repel fleas and were often burned or strewn on the floors for that reason – anything with the word *pulicaria* or *pulegium* (from the Latin *pulex*, a flea) in its botanical name, such as fleabane (*Pulicaria dysenterica*) and pennyroyal (*Mentha pulegium*), tells you that its purpose was to control fleas. The Latin name *tinctoria* indicates a dyer's plant – for example, dyer's greenweed (*Genista tinctoria*) and woad (*Isatis tinctoria*).

Types of cottage garden flowers

Cottage garden flowers cover an enormous range of plant families and usage groups.

Bee plants are those that naturally produce large amounts of nectar and these were deliberately grown by early cottagers who, not being able to afford sugar, kept hives for honey. Good bee plants include old-fashioned hardy annuals, such as calendula, herbs – particularly marjoram and borage – and old-fashioned flowers such as lavender and comfrey (*Symphytum*). Those that flower very early, such as *Pulmonaria rubra*, are very worthwhile, as bees first emerge early in spring when relatively few flowers are out.

Plants that attract bees also tend to be those that are good for attracting butterflies and beneficial insects like hoverflies, so bee plants are now back in favour for natural, wildlife-friendly and organic gardens.

Herbs are thought of as culinary plants nowadays, but in the past they were loosely considered to be anything with a household use. Herbs were used medicinally, and for making toiletries and cleaning products of all kinds. Scented herbs were strewn on the floor along with rushes to kill smells and could be swept up and replaced as necessary. Herbs were also used for dying home-spun fabrics; the preparation of herbs for dying is long and involved, and the dyes often produce colours quite unlike those of the flowers.

Edible crops were once the mainstay of 'real' cottage gardens, but since Victorian times vegetables have often been grown ornamentally with flowers. Indeed, runner beans and tomatoes were originally introduced as ornamental plants. Cardoon, globe artichoke and Jerusalem artichoke make structural additions to the back of a large flower border; squashes, gourds and climbing beans look attractive grown over arches; purple dwarf French beans, coloured varieties of lettuce and frilly parsley make evocative decorative edgings to paths.

Vegetables grow better in rows, but a traditional vegetable patch can nevertheless be enlivened by the addition of rows of flowers for cutting or for use as edible garnishes.

Hardy annuals are those that grow in spring, flower the same summer, and die after setting seed. A lot of the most authentic cottage garden flowers are the more aggressive self-seeders that pop up uninvited all over the garden, even among clumps of other plants. The reason they do so well is that without being transplanted they grow a wide-spreading root system, which enables the plant to survive without watering when pot-grown plants or transplanted seedlings, with their confined or injured root systems, need regular attention.

Biennials are considered very old fashioned and hardly figure in modern gardens at all as they are 'inconvenient', but in a cottage-style situation they behave very much like hardy annuals, with their one year of life taking place from summer to summer – they grow one year and flower the next. A number of the plants we grow as biennials these days – notably wallflowers and sweet Williams – are technically short-lived perennials, which we find more convenient to pull up after flowering and replace each year.

Perennials are by far the biggest single group of cottage garden flowers. They include a number of subgroups, all loosely known as old-fashioned flowers.

Florists' flowers are enthusiasts' plants, such as violets, pinks (*Dianthus*) and primroses, which were first grown as far back as the 17th century.

Many immediate relatives of **native wildflowers** have become old cottage classics. There are double forms of celandine, meadow cranesbill, buttercup, red campion and lady's smock, plus decorative forms of native plants, such as curled tansy (*Tanacetum vulgare* var. *crispum*), whose plain-leaved relative was once wrapped around meat as a precaution against maggots.

Introduced species, brought to this country long ago but left largely unimproved, such as Jerusalem cross (*Lychnis chalcedonica*) and Madonna lily (*Lilium candidum*), are another important group of cottage garden perennials.

Woody plants like trees and shrubs would mainly have been represented in old cottage gardens by mixed hedges of native species, such as hazel, blackthorn (*Prunus spinosa*) and fruit trees and bushes, none of which really qualify as flowers, although nowadays old-fashioned roses and clematis are among our most popular cottage garden flowers. Ornamental forms of fruit and nut trees, such as crab apples and contorted hazel (*Corylus avellana* 'Contorta'), are often grown in today's gardens for height, shape, structure or out-of-season interest, and most people will also grow at least a few non-traditional plants, such as winter-flowering *Lonicera* × *purpusii* or red-stemmed dogwoods (*Cornus alba* 'Sibirica') to extend the season of interest.

Old-fashioned roses are probably not 'old' in cottage gardens, although early cottagers may well have had wild rose species, such as dog rose (*Rosa canina*), growing in the mixed hedges that often surrounded their gardens. The roses we loosely call 'old fashioned' today include some true species such as Rosa Mundi (correctly, *Rosa gallica* 'Versicolor') and their cultivars; shrub roses, which often include some quite modern introductions; and old roses that were mainly bred around 150 years ago, when roses came into fashion in 'proper' gardens. What suits them to cottage gardens is that they look 'old' due to the shape of the flowers, and they have a short flowering season more like shrubs than modern bush roses, which lends them to being underplanted with bulbs and cottage flowers, instead of grown in formal rose beds with bare soil underneath.

Climbers in old cottage gardens would mainly have been represented by native honeysuckle (*Lonicera periclymenum*) and traveller's joy (*Clematis vitalba*), but nowadays climbers are an essential part of the 'layered' cottage garden planting style. Today's fashionable hybrid clematis look the part and have the right growth habit to suit cottage gardens, and modern owners find them a very acceptable way of adding a colourful 'top layer' to a traditionally congested, multi-storey garden by growing them through trees and shrubs. Because of their sparse foliage they cast little shade, which makes them well suited to growing through other climbers, such as rambler roses on arches and along fences.

Old fashioned roses are the stars of early summer, but because of their short flowering season, it's essential to have plenty of other flowers to cover the rest of the season.

Growing cottage garden flowers

The original cottage gardeners practised a very different kind of gardening from the type that took place at the 'Big Manor House', where skilled, trained gardeners did everything by the book. Cottage gardening – at least, cottage flower gardening – was based on minimal intervention.

Soil

From a self-sufficient cottager's point of view, the important part of the garden was the vegetable patch. Any manure (from the pigsty in the back garden) would have been reserved for productive plants rather than 'wasted' on flowers. Despite that, flower gardens could be surprisingly rich and fertile, even without conventional soil improvement. Cottages were often rebuilt on the site of much earlier hovels, so the ground around them could have been in regular use for very many years, housing a variety of livestock, vegetable gardens and the portable privies that were regularly moved around the garden.

Since flower beds were filled with a solid carpet of permanent plants, it was not possible to improve the ground even if the owners had wanted to. Some soil improvement would have happened accidentally by 'leakage' from paths, which were made by tipping cinders and ash from the fire anywhere the householder needed to walk, in order to prevent regularly used routes deteriorating into muddy puddles in wet weather. The paths were topped up as they were trodden in, and new ones made as the garden layout changed, so over a long period of time more open-textured material would gradually

Old cottage garden flowers are the sort that do not need staking or regular splitting.

lighten the soil, providing some aeration and drainage as well as nutrients such as potash. Cottagers also used the silt cleared from farm ditches in winter to top dress their flower beds – much like mulching today – and this would have been particularly beneficial for the type of flowers that 'grow themselves out of the ground', such as London pride (*Saxifraga* × *urbium*) and some types of hardy cranesbill (*Geranium*).

Today, few people have the type of cottage garden that was still around at the turn of the last century, where plants were just stuck in and left to fend for themselves – but then we are mostly not gardening in soil that has been in continuous cultivation for generations, nor restricting ourselves to the relatively small range of old cottage plants that grow themselves. We have to start the ball rolling by following modern soil improvement, to produce the good growing conditions needed for today's cottage gardens. A couple of compost heaps are essential for recycling garden waste as bulky organic matter to prepare new ground for flower beds, and for providing a regular supply of mulching material.

SITING

Originally, cottage garden flower beds were put where they were most convenient, which generally meant on any odd bits of ground that could not be used for something more important.

Traditionally, a small front garden would contain a continuous carpet of cottage flowers, with a straight path running through it from the garden gate to the front door. If the vegetable patch was located at the side of the house instead of around the back there might be a narrow flower bed along the most visible side of it, and garden paths – which were mostly kept as straight as possible – would have narrow flower beds running along either side of them. Nobody worried much about choosing the place that was best for the plants; any that did not like the conditions simply died out, and their place was soon taken over by those that did find things to their liking. But then, early cottage gardeners did not have to pay for their plants.

In today's gardens, flower beds are usually placed with an eye to the overall design of the garden; gardeners assess the growing conditions in terms of sun and shade, soil type and so on, and choose plants that suit particular places. Enthusiasts, however, will often do it the other way round; they start from the premise that they want to grow particular plants, such as pinks (*Dianthus*), and then find a place where the conditions are right to make a bed specially for them.

A traditional cottage front garden is wall-to-wall flowers with just a straight path from the gate to the front door, and no grass. The same style works for modern gardens where you need parking space for a car.

Cottage garden flowers cover such a wide range of plants that it is possible to find something that will grow in just about any set of garden conditions, but for the vast majority the ideal situation is one that gets sun for half the day or more, is well sheltered, and has good fertile soil that drains freely but contains plenty of organic matter so that it retains moisture.

Plants for light shade

Astrantia	*Geranium*
Brunnera	*Helleborus*
Buxus	*Narcissus*
Dicentra	*Polygonatum*
Euphorbia amygdaloides	*Primula*
E. griffithii cultivars	*Pulmonaria*

Plants tolerant of deeper shade

Euphorbia amygdaloides 'Robbiae'	*Iris foetidissima*
	Lunaria annua
Geranium phaeum	*Viola odorata* cultivars

Plants for sun

Dianthus	*Rosmarinus*
Erysimum	*Salvia officinalis* and cultivars
Iris	*Sedum spectabile*
Lavandula	*Sempervivum*
Lychnis coronaria	*Thymus* cultivars
L. chalcedonica	Roses

PLANNING

To achieve the traditional congested look without the 'hit and miss' planting of the past, a modern cottage garden is best planned in a series of layers. Trees and evergreens will form a year-round framework to flowering shrubs, such as old roses underplanted with perennials, which in turn are underplanted with carpets of spring bulbs. The traditional planting 'rule' is tallest to the back, shortest to the front, so the flowers graduate upwards in size, allowing everything to be seen.

A generously stocked cottage garden offers plenty of possibilities for creative plant associations. It is a good idea to stand new plants in place temporarily while you consider their impact on the rest of the garden before planting them. As a general rule, a group of plants containing one spiky, upright shape, one rounded, bushy shape and one horizontal, ground-hugging shape usually works well. Unless you are limiting yourself to a colour scheme of, say, purple, mauve and pink or yellow, white and grey, where nothing will clash, it is advisable to include plenty of foliage plants, such as heucheras and pulmonarias, to break up potentially offending colours.

Making a new bed

It is essential to get rid of perennial weeds from cottage garden flower beds, as they are impossible to tackle once a good carpet of plants is established. If weeds like bindweed or ground elder are present, start on soil preparation a good six months before you plan to plant, so that they can be thoroughly dug out. Alternatively, use a glyphosate weedkiller when weed growth is strong, and repeat every time new growth appears; two or three doses at roughly six- to eight-week intervals should be enough to tackle even well-established problem weeds, as long as they are not allowed to recover between treatments. If the soil has been under grass, strip off the turf to a depth of 4cm (1½in) to remove any roots capable of regenerating, then stack the turves upside down and leave them for a year to break down into good fibrous loam, which is invaluable for top dressing.

Once you have cleared the ground, dig it over well, incorporating as much well-rotted manure, garden compost, rotted straw or whatever you can obtain as locally as possible. Double digging is usually recommended as it gives plants a deeper rooting area, but is only worth doing if the soil is naturally deep. On shallow chalky or stony soil where the subsoil is even worse, or on heavy clay where there is sticky yellow or blue stodge a spade's depth down, it is much better not to mix this with the topsoil, so single dig only. Clay soil can be improved a good deal by digging in sharp sand, fine grit, coarse bark chippings and even shellfish shells to open up the texture and improve the drainage. Organic matter does much the same job, but only temporarily as it rots away to nothing after a few years, whereas 'hard' materials last much better.

Planting

It is not often you get the opportunity to plant a whole new bed from scratch in an established cottage garden. Choose plants that will look good together and enjoy similar growing conditions, then stand them on the prepared soil, still in their pots, while you arrange them. The traditional style is for plants to be spaced rather closer together than usual, so that they quickly cover all the bare soil. The idea is to fit as many plants into the space as possible, in order to pack as much colour and interest into as small an area as you can.

To plant a new bed, use a trowel to make planting holes slightly larger than the pot in which each plant is growing. Tip the plants out of their pots and set them in position, so that the top of the rootball lies roughly level with the surface of the surrounding soil; then fill the remaining hole with topsoil, firm lightly, and water in. Spring is the best planting time, so that new plants have time to make some growth before they are expected to flower, but in practice a lot of people prefer to plant new beds during the summer when plants are in flower, so that they get a better feel for the eventual effect. It is perfectly acceptable to plant during the growing season, provided all the plants are pot-grown so that they suffer only minimal root disturbance, and they are kept well watered afterwards.

Although it is rare to make new beds in an established cottage garden, adding new plants to existing beds is a very common practice. Very often, an existing bed is enlarged to make room for more plants, in which case the turf should be stripped from the area and the soil improved in exactly the same way as when creating a new bed. Equally, following a visit to a nursery or show, impulse purchases will be slotted in between other plants in an existing bed, in the same way that old cottage gardeners would have found room to grow a 'slip' that their neighbour had passed over the fence. As long as the ground was well prepared when the original bed was made, only the planting hole itself needs to be prepared. Make a hole two or three times the size of the pot in which the new plant is growing, fork some well-rotted compost and a sprinkling of general purpose fertiliser into the bottom, and then plant the new addition. When planting during the growing season, avoid breaking up the rootball any more than is absolutely necessary. With a seriously pot-bound plant, it is a good idea to unravel some of the outer layer of coiled roots so they can proceed outwards into the surrounding soil, but otherwise just plant the whole rootball intact.

AFTERCARE

Traditionally, cottage garden flowers were left fairly well alone once they had been planted. A dense carpet of spreading and self-seeding flowers would quickly cover the ground in spring and smother out annual weeds, and due to generations of good cultivation there were no perennial weeds. The only nourishment that most flowers received was a top dressing of silt, removed when the ditches from the surrounding farmland were cleared out in winter.

Nowadays, common practice is to apply a mulch over all exposed soil each spring, before perennials have had time to cover the ground. The mulch replenishes the organic reserves and moisture-holding capacity of the soil, and helps to smother out annual weeds before a carpet of perennials can do the job. If you have a supply of fibrous topsoil, made by stacking upturned turves for a year, this is best used for top dressing plants such as heucheras and those *Geranium* species that produce a network of thick stems resting above the ground. Work the material down into these plants with your fingers, so that the stems are protected from drying out and to encourage stem rooting. Cottage garden flowers do not require high levels of nutrients, but if background fertility is not naturally good it pays to apply a light dose of general purpose fertiliser at the same time as mulching, in spring.

However, since few modern cottage gardeners like the totally random, overgrown look of a real old cottage garden, nowadays it is normal to treat cottage flower beds and borders in very much the same way as modern herbaceous borders. Mulch and feed in spring, and lift and divide overgrown plants in spring or autumn so that adjacent clumps do not run into each other. Weed out unwanted self-sown seedlings as necessary, or pot up to grow on and replant where they are needed later, rather than leaving the border to 'design itself'. Choice plants will need individual attention according to their particular requirements.

CONTAINER GROWING

Working cottage gardeners of centuries ago would have had little time for looking after outdoor containers, but they grew a few pots of flowers on the windowsill indoors. Since cottages were unheated, the choice of plants was limited to nearly hardy kinds. Mint was often grown in the kitchen to repel flies, and plants like mother-of-thousands (*Saxifraga stolonifera*), aspidistra, mignonette (*Reseda odorata*) and *Campanula isophylla* were grown in living rooms. Pelargoniums became popular cottage windowsill flowers, surviving winter as dried-out stumps kept in a store room. My grandmother had some very splendid ancient, gnarled cyclamen corms that lived for many years on her deep windowsills and reached the size of saucers, in 30cm (12in) pots of garden soil.

Nowadays, outdoor containers are considered very 'cottagey'. For authenticity, recycle old containers, such as old stone sinks, second-hand clay pots, old metal buckets and leaky household pots and pans, but modern containers, such as plastic or glazed ceramic pots and wire-framed hanging baskets do not look out of place once they are full of flowers.

Cottage garden flowers for containers

Many of the more compact kinds of hardy annuals are suitable for growing in cottage containers. Short varieties of sunflowers and stocks, and bushy varieties of nasturtiums are particularly suitable for pots, while trailing nasturtiums, canary creeper (*Tropaeolum peregrinum*) and knee-high types of sweet peas all make good flowers for hanging baskets. The great advantage of growing cottage annuals in containers is that the seeds can be sown straight into the container in early to mid-spring, with no need for a greenhouse. Line hanging baskets with moss or artificial liners and fill with lightweight, soilless (but peat-free) potting compost, which can also be used for free-standing containers on the ground. Sow large seeds like sweet peas and nasturtiums 5cm (2in) apart, then press them individually just below the surface of the compost. Sprinkle smaller seeds very thinly all over the surface, then cover to their own depth with more compost. You can thin them out later if they come up too thickly. Water newly sown seeds lightly, and keep the containers

Containers are handy for filling gaps in the garden where earlier flowers have finished, as well as for standing on paths or paving.

in a sheltered spot – they can even be left by the back door or wherever you want them to flower, so that you do not have to move them later. Alternatively, sow the seeds in small pots or trays in a cold frame or greenhouse or on the windowsill of a cool room indoors, and set young plants into containers just before they start flowering.

Old-fashioned hardy annuals start flowering slightly earlier but stop sooner than modern bedding plants, so by late summer cottage containers will be coming to an end. However, this is a good time to replant them with pansies, polyanthus, double forms of *Bellis perennis*, wallflowers or spring bulbs, for an early spring display of cottage flowers.

As an alternative to annuals, which need to be replanted twice a year, some of the more compact **cottage garden perennials** can be grown all year round in containers, although they may need to be moved to an out-of-the-way spot for the winter when they look dead. Choose cottage flowers that are naturally compact, with a long flowering season and good foliage; reasonable drought tolerance is another useful asset.

Good kinds include pinks (*Dianthus*), evergreen herbs, such as rosemaries and thymes, *Alchemilla mollis*, *Lysimachia nummularia* and rock-plant relatives like *Arabis, Sempervivum, Campanula portenschlagiana, Sedum acre*, thrift (*Armeria maritima*), *Erinus* and *Erigeron*. Plant containers in spring, using John Innes No. 2 or 3 potting compost, with one type of plant per pot; alternatively, group together several kinds that require similar growing conditions in a larger container.

Lilies are also good for growing in pots, but again the more compact varieties are the most suitable. Plant them in spring, putting three bulbs in a 38cm (15in) pot of John Innes No. 3 and placing them close to the bottom of the container, as most lilies need to be planted deeply. Water sparingly to start with, and increase the amount given steadily as the plants grow. Apply diluted liquid tomato feed regularly during the summer, as lilies are heavy feeders in autumn. Decrease watering and stop feeding as the leaves start to die down, and either plant the bulbs in the garden or leave them in their pots in a shed so they do not freeze solid during the winter, repotting into fresh compost the following spring. This may sound extravagant – but it's necessary.

Clematis are also very good plants for growing in containers; again, it is the smaller-growing kinds with a long flowering season that are most suitable. Plant one clematis in a large tub or 38–45cm (15–18in) pot of John Innes No. 3 in spring, and train the stems up a rustic structure or simple obelisk. Clematis in containers need regular watering and, being greedy plants, should be fed every two weeks from spring to late summer with diluted liquid tomato feed. In winter, the plants can be left outside as long as there is no risk of the compost freezing solid – during prolonged cold spells, move them temporarily to a more sheltered spot or insulate them.

Clematis pruning is easy in containers. Varieties that normally need heavy pruning should be cut back to just above the top of the container, while those that are not normally pruned are best given a light tidy-up – just enough to reshape them and get rid of straggly old growth. Each spring, top dress by scraping away the top 2.5cm (1in) or so of old potting compost and replacing it with new material to which some

You can get away with a big mixture of colours in a cottage garden as long as you include plenty of foliage – green flowers can also be useful.

slow-release fertiliser has been added. Otherwise, despite regular liquid feeding the plants will run short of nutrients and will not flower so freely.

For real enthusiasts, **florists' flowers**, such as auriculas and violets, make perfect cottage container plants, grown singly in 8–10cm (3–4in) pots. When flowering is over, remove the plants from display and keep them in a shady cold frame, with the pots plunged to their rims in damp sand to maintain evenly cool, moist roots.

For specialist plants like these, enthusiasts often prefer to make up their own potting mixtures based on leafmould (made by composting fallen autumn leaves, which are damped and packed in perforated plastic sacks for a year until they are decomposed) and fibrous loam (made by stacking a pile of turf for a year until the grass is dead and only crumbly 'rooty' soil remains). You can also make quite a good version using a mixture of John Innes No. 2 potting compost and coir, which has much the same function as leafmould in potting mixtures.

It is usual to repot these plants every year so the clumps that build up during the summer can be separated into single plants, which look more traditional and have bigger flowers all growing in the centre of the plant. Regular division also keeps the plants vigorous – they have a nasty habit of dying out if left to themselves for too long.

Windowboxes are normally planted with a succession of annual bedding plants. Choose trailing varieties, such as nasturtiums, trailing fuchsias, lobelia or ivy-leaved pelargoniums, and low, compact plants like argyranthemums that will not seriously restrict the view from inside the house, making rooms dark and preventing the windows from opening.

PROPAGATING COTTAGE GARDEN FLOWERS

Early cottage gardeners, from necessity, raised all their own plants, and everything had to be propagated in the easiest possible way since they did not have greenhouses, heated propagators, or even things like hormone rooting powder, cling film and plastic bags, which gardening enthusiasts take so much for granted today.

Although nowadays it is easy enough to go out and buy just about any plants you might want, it is much more satisfying to grow as many of your own as possible. And, since cottage gardening is a very sociable activity, part of the fun lies in swapping plants with friends and providing stock for plant sales tables at fundraising events.

In any case, propagation is good cottage gardening practice. The more short-lived cottage flowers need to be propagated regularly if you are to keep them, and in the case of unusual plants that are hard to replace it is always wise to propagate them as an insurance against losses.

Division

The quickest and easiest way to make a new plant is to split up an old one. Moreover, division is an ideal method of propagation, as it gives you new flowering-sized plants virtually

33

instantly, with a very low failure rate. This method can only be used for clump-forming perennials and you can only produce a few new plants from each parent, so it is of little use to the nurseryman; however, the divisons are genetically identical to their parents, so at home this is a good method for propagating named varieties that you want to keep true to type.

The best time to divide a plant is in spring or autumn, at either end of the main growing season. Dig up the whole plant and chop the clump into several smaller chunks using a sharp spade. You can use the same method to divide an old plant in order to rejuvenate it. In this case, replant the youngest pieces from the edge and discard the old pieces from the centre.

Many of the more rugged, spreading cottage garden plants, however, can keep creeping almost indefinitely, and rarely if ever need dividing, so if you want a spare piece to give to a friend, you can simply take a spade and slice a chunk from the growing plant at almost any time of year. If there is a lot of top growth, the division will take best if you trim it back to 8–10cm (3–4in) high and remove any flowering stems. As long as the soil is well prepared in the new planting place and the division is kept well watered until it re-establishes itself, you will usually be successful.

You can also divide newly bought plants growing in pots at almost any time from spring to autumn, as long as there is a good potful with several stems. Simply tip the plant out of the pot, work your fingers into a natural gap in the growth and gently tear the rootball apart, leaving each division roughly the same size and with plenty of roots. Fair-sized divisions produced in this way can be planted straight out into the garden, but small pieces are best potted and grown on until they are big enough to plant out.

Cuttings

Cuttings are a convenient way to produce a huge range of perennial cottage garden flowers. As with division, cuttings produce new plants that are genetically identical to their parent, so this method of propagation is another one to use for named varieties. However, cuttings take longer to produce planting-sized specimens.

There are several different types of cuttings, used for plants with different growth habits, but only stem and basal cuttings are applicable to cottage garden flowers.

Stem cuttings, also known as **tip cuttings**, are the most widely used kind. They are made from the soft tips of actively growing young stems during the growing season, at any time from late spring to late summer, and pelargonium cuttings are a good example. To make stem cuttings, snip 10–15cm (4–6in) lengths from the ends of the current year's shoots using secateurs. Non-flowering shoots make the best propagating material, but in the case of plants with a very long flowering season, such as pelargoniums, this is not always possible, so when preparing the cutting remove any flowers or buds to reduce water loss. Remove the lower leaves from the cutting for the same reason, and make a clean cut immediately beneath the lowest node (leaf joint) to remove any damaged or bruised tissue that might otherwise rot. Some gardeners like to dip the wounded ends of stem cuttings into hormone rooting powder, which contains fungicide as well as rooting hormones, but with subjects that will root quickly and easily this is not really necessary.

Pelargoniums, or 'geraniums' as they are popularly called, are one of the easiest plants to grow from tip cuttings. It always pays to take more cuttings than you need, to allow for losses.

Push the cuttings that you have prepared into containers of seed compost, roughly to their half-way point. Water them just enough to moisten the compost evenly and settle the base of the cuttings in place. Plants with soft or thin leaves, such as fuchsias, will root best in a humid atmosphere, so push a short piece of split cane into the middle of the container and slip a large, loose plastic bag over the top to serve as a makeshift propagator. In contrast, plants that have a natural resistance to drought – including those with furry, aromatic or silvery leaves, such as rosemary, pinks and artemisia – will root best when open to the air and may rot in a humid atmosphere.

Basal cuttings are made from shoots that grow from the base of a spreading or clump-forming perennial plant that, for some reason, does not propagate well from tip cuttings – it may produce weak and spindly growth, or stems with tips that are nothing but flowers. Good examples of plants that need to be propagated from basal cuttings are geranium species, delphiniums and lupins.

This type of cutting can only be taken in spring, when the parent plants first start back into growth and the first short shoots have grown 8–10cm (3–4in) above the ground. Carefully clear away the soil and any mulching material from the neck of the parent plant, to expose as much as possible of the base of the stems. Cut away a few shoots cleanly from the parent, as low down as possible, and treat them in the same way as tip cuttings. If it is possible to detach some shoots complete with existing roots, dig these away from the parent plant using a trowel and pot them up without further preparation as 'Irishman's cuttings'. Once the pots are full of roots, which often takes only a few weeks, the young plants can be set out in the garden.

Basal cuttings can also be taken from tuberous plants, notably dahlias and chocolate cosmos (*Cosmos atrosanguineus*), by starting the tubers into growth in a heated greenhouse or on a windowsill indoors and using the first shoots that appear as cuttings. With tuberous plants it is essential to propagate them early in the season, so that the young plants have time to form new tubers that are large enough to enable them to survive a long spell of dormancy during the winter.

Sowing seed

Growing plants from seed is an immensely satisfying pastime, and it is a useful way to acquire unusual plants that are not readily available in any other way. Seed raising is the best method of propagation for anyone who wants to produce a large number of the same type of plants, particularly annuals.

The technique you need to use varies according to the type of seeds you are sowing.

Hardy annuals are traditionally sown in spring, to flower later the same summer. You can sow them either directly into the ground where they are to flower or in trays for transplanting later, rather like bedding plants.

If you want to sow annuals direct, it is absolutely essential that you have good, fertile, weed-free soil. Prepare the ground by digging in plenty of well-rotted organic matter in the autumn or winter; then, as soon as the soil becomes workable in spring, remove any weeds and rake well, then mark out the area where each type of seed is to be sown and sow by broadcasting the seeds over each patch. When the seedlings emerge, thin them out to a few centimetres apart so that the resulting plants cover the ground without being overcrowded.

If the ground is well populated with weed seeds, it is much safer to sow the seeds in rows in a nursery bed or the vegetable patch, so that you can distinguish the flower seedlings from the weeds. Thin them out, then transplant to their flowering positions when they are big enough to move.

The other method is to sow the seeds in trays of seed compost, thin out the seedlings, and then plant out in their flowering positions when they are big enough to handle and the ground is in workable condition. However, now that mild winters are becoming more usual, it is worth taking the risk of sowing some of the tougher hardy annuals such as nasturtiums, Californian poppy (*Eschscholzia*), and *Cerinthe major* in autumn (a common practice in the south of France for many years), so that they start flowering earlier.

Biennials can be sown in all the same ways as annuals – in the open ground, or in seed trays or pots in a cold frame or greenhouse – but should be sown later, from late spring to midsummer. Thin out or pot up the seedlings, and then plant them out in their flowering positions in autumn, when they are big enough and space is available.

Perennials can be sown in rows outside in early to midsummer, but since packets contain relatively few seeds these are probably worth sowing in more controlled conditions, in pots in a greenhouse. Perennials sown with heat in midwinter will often flower the same summer; otherwise, sow in late spring or early summer and prick out the seedlings into individual pots. Grow on the young plants under glass until autumn or the following spring, when they can be planted out in the garden.

Sources of seed

Seed catalogues from all the major companies list a good range of cottage garden flowers, and they are well illustrated with colour photographs so that you can see what you are getting. Smaller or more specialised seed firms often list a greater number of varieties of cottage garden flowers, herbs and wildflowers, but without pictures. A large range of seeds is also available to members of the Royal Horticultural Society from the gardens at Wisley, and specialist societies, such as the Hardy Plant Society and the Cottage Garden Society each organize seed exchanges for their members.

It is well worth **saving your own seed** to donate to society seed exchanges or to propagate spare plants for replacements, sales or swaps. However, it is only worth saving seeds of pure species and old-fashioned open-pollinated varieties of annuals, as hybrids do not come true from seed.

To save seed, keep an eye on suitable plants with developing seed capsules or pods, and when they are nearly ripe place a paper bag over the top and fix it with an elastic band. In this way, when the seed ripens you will not lose the seeds if the capsules or pods open and shed the contents before you can get to them. Otherwise, pick the seedheads as they turn beige, place them in paper bags – one for each type of plant – and hang them up in a cool, dark, dry place.

If the capsules or pods have not opened and shed their seeds naturally you will need to open them up when they have dried out completely and extract the seeds by hand. Leave the seeds out in the air to finish drying thoroughly, then store in plain paper envelopes. Do not use plastic bags, as these will sweat – the resulting humidity causes fungal infections to build up in the seed, which may not germinate. Most home-saved seed is best sown either as soon as it is ripe or the following spring.

If they are not deadheaded, many cottage garden flowers

shed copious amounts of seed during the season, resulting in **self-sown seedlings** appearing all around the garden. Particularly prolific are purple fennel (*Foeniculum vulgare* 'Purpureum'), cerinthe, wallflowers, verbascums, foxgloves, violas, *Verbena bonariensis* and *V. officinalis*, love-in-a-mist (*Nigella damascena*), aquilegias, borage, geranium and euphorbia species, honesty (*Lunaria annua*), valerian, hellebores and any number of hardy annuals.

Foxgloves self-seed very freely, which looks delightful between trees, but in a border they tend to smother neighbouring flowers and take over unless you thin them out severely.

Traditionally, cottage gardeners simply left self-sown seedlings to grow where they came up naturally, and you can still do this – although the result is the very random, chaotic, overcrowded garden typical of a century or more ago. If you like a rather more orderly scene, it is worth pulling out self-sown seedlings that appear where you do not want them, leaving only those that are well placed. Any excess seedlings can be potted up for replanting in more appropriate positions later, or to be used for plant sales at garden events.

Some cottage garden flowers, such as cerinthe and purple fennel, come reasonably true from seed, but plants like hellebores, violas and aquilegias often take the opportunity to cross with other varieties in the immediate area and the result is a mixture of mongrels, some that will be nothing special, while others have good colours or other characteristics that make them well worth keeping. The only way to find out is to grow them, so either leave them in situ or transplant to a nursery bed until they reach flowering size. In the case of plants, such as hellebores, that dislike root disturbance once they are mature, put self-sown seedlings in pots so they can be planted out later if the results are worth keeping.

Coping with problems

Cottage garden flowers generally suffer from few problems, which is one of the reasons why they have remained popular through the centuries to become cottage classics. Several serious problems have reached the UK in recent years, however. Notable arrivals include chrysanthemum white rust, pelargonium rust, antirrhinum rust, hollyhock rust and acanthus powdery mildew. A couple of hundred years of plant breeding and selection have also given us varieties of cottage garden flowers that are different from the ones in the original cottager's garden, superior in many ways but often more susceptible to pests and diseases. This is particularly true of roses, which are notorious for black spot, mildew and rust.

Cottage gardeners of old would have faced their fair share of problems, however, and they would have been forced to turn to natural or physical remedies as they did not have the means to buy or apply the types of chemicals that are available today.

Overcrowding is a common occurrence in typically congested cottage gardens. When plants of equal size and growth rate are planted close together, they usually manage to 'fight it out among themselves' quite well. However, when small or slow plants are grown alongside aggressive, fast-spreading kinds, the good doers quickly swamp everything in their path, while the rest gradually die out due to lack of light, fungal disease, or competition for water and nutrients. The solution is to grow together only plants of similar growth rates that need

similar conditions, and not to plant out new plants into the garden until they are big enough to fend for themselves. Small, young plants – even those of quite vigorous species – may not survive being overshadowed by fast-growing neighbours. It pays to visit newly planted flowers regularly, and if necessary hold back neighbouring plants with sticks until the newcomers are well established.

Tall flowers are not staked in cottage gardens unless it's really necessary – a slight lean looks far more romantic.

Slugs and snails are some of the commonest garden pests, now that mild winters allow them to be active all year long. All sorts of remedies have been used against them, with varying degrees of success. Slug pellets are an option, but a lot of people prefer not to use them. Placing pest-proof barriers of holly leaves or rings of soot around at-risk plants is a traditional method, the biggest problem being that they need to be topped up regularly. However, there is a good range of modern remedies that are quite effective, even without resorting to slug pellets. Large garden centres and companies that supply organic remedies by mail order sell moisture-absorbing minerals, which are placed in a ring around susceptible plants to dehydrate molluscs attempting to crawl over the top; products containing aluminium sulphate can be sprinkled on the soil, and copper tapes can be placed around the rims of pots. Alternatively pathogenic nematodes, available by mail order from suppliers of biological controls, can be watered on to pots or garden soil for biological control of slugs, although they are not very effective against snails.

Greenfly, or aphids, may be less of a problem in gardens where chemicals are not normally used, as the resident population of blue tits and beneficial insects such as hoverflies, ladybirds, lacewings and parasitic wasps give a reasonable degree of control. The natural enemies of aphids will destroy them in large numbers, but the populations of beneficial insects often build up after the population of aphids, so that the control appears after the damage is done. It is not usually necessary to control aphids chemically, but for aphids on roses, a product called Roseclear 2 is currently available, which contains pirimicarb – an insecticide specific for aphids; it will not kill natural enemies. Roseclear 2 also contains fungicides and can be used on other plants to control rusts and mildews. So-called organic insecticides, which are based on plant products, fatty acids or oils, have a wide activity and do kill beneficial insects as well as aphids. However, if large numbers of greenfly are seen congregating on the tips of young shoots, a simple remedy is to wipe them off between your fingers or with a damp cloth.

Vine weevil affects primulas and cyclamen particularly badly, but now that it is so widespread it will also attack other young plants especially those in containers. Where it is a regular problem, the best remedy is to use the appropriate nematode in late summer for the biological control of the fat, white, C-shaped underground larvae that devour the roots. For container

Because cottage gardens contain such a wide mixture of species, they encourage beneficial insects, which take care of pests for you – as long as you don't insist on having absolutely perfect plants.

grown ornamental plants, there is the alternative of watering the compost with imidacloprid (Bio Provado Vine Weevil Killer). Imidacloprid-amended potting compost is also available. Kill adult weevils by hand whenever they are seen, to reduce the population.

Rust appears on roses, hollyhocks, comfrey (*Symphytum*), antirrhinums, chrysanthemums and pelargoniums in particular. The type of rust that affects one plant will not spread to others, but rusts are difficult to eliminate once they are established. Cut back and destroy affected foliage, keep susceptible plants well fed and watered in summer, so they do not suffer from stress, and if particular varieties of roses are always affected it is worth destroying them and substituting with varieties that have better natural disease resistance. Fungicides will also control rusts. If you try to control hollyhock or chrysanthemum rust by picking off infected leaves, you will often end up with a very poor plant.

Powdery mildew is commonplace on roses, honeysuckle and pulmonarias, causing foliage to look as if it has been dusted with talcum powder, and eventually to turn brown and die. Mildew normally occurs in mid- to late summer, particularly on plants that have been under stress due to shortage of water. In the case of honeysuckle, plants growing on walls are especially at risk, as the foundations absorb a lot of moisture from the soil, while the wall itself deflects rain, so the ground is often very dry. Treat susceptible plants before symptoms appear by feeding well and mulching heavily in spring, and keep the ground watered during very dry weather to avoid stress to plants; if possible, water affected plants well to try to avoid symptoms worsening. When badly affected by mildew, pulmonarias and other small perennials can be cut back close to ground level and, after watering well, healthy new growth will quickly appear. Use fungicides to assist when these methods fail.

In the case of roses, feed and mulch well in spring, and if mildew and black spot are regular problems look for varieties known to have better disease resistance. Dig plenty of organic matter deeply into the ground to retain moisture and nutrients before planting the new roses.

COTTAGE FLOWERS IN THE GARDEN

It is not essential to have a traditional cottage garden in order to grow cottage garden flowers, or to grow them in the same way as you see them in prints of old photographs. In fact, there are various ways of incorporating old favourites into any reasonably traditional, densely planted style of garden.

THE COTTAGE GARDEN BORDER

This is the cottage garden version of the mixed border. In an old cottage garden, a large border often contained a row of fruit trees or gooseberry bushes underplanted with a mixture of shade-tolerate spring bulbs and flowers, or there may have been a continuous carpet of flowers growing in front of a mixed country hedge containing a range of fruit and nut trees.

Today, ornamental forms of fruit and nut trees such as crab apples or quinces (*Cydonia*), contorted hazel (*Corylus avellana* 'Contorta'), and traditional cottage garden shrubs, such as hardy fuchsias, chaenomeles, forsythia, winter jasmine or shrub roses are more likely to be used to make a background for cottage garden flowers. Carpets of spring bulbs and climbers, such as honeysuckle, clematis and climbing roses are added to extend the season of interest.

Traditional low-maintenance border

This is the same type of feature that appeared in old cottage gardens, where time for leisure gardening was very limited. The plants used are the very easy-going kinds: self-seeding hardy annuals and vigorous, spreading perennials, which can

To ensure a long continuous flowering season, a modern cottage garden needs a bit of everything – trees, shrubs, roses, climbers, perennials, annuals and bulbs.

fight it out among themselves and form a dense carpet of plants that covers the ground completely by late spring, smothering out weeds. Good plants to team together in this way include bluebells, hardy cranesbills (*Geranium*), comfrey (*Symphytum*), love-in-a-mist (*Nigella damascena*), nasturtiums and, for contrast, foliage plants such as gardener's garters (*Phalaris arundinacea* var. *picta*). It is essential to avoid introducing more delicate plants, as they will not stand the competition.

Plant the perennials 60–90cm (2–3ft) apart, and plant or sow annuals between them; after the first season a little weeding will be necessary beyond late spring; however, you will need to weed out excess self-sown seedlings and any that come up where they are not wanted. A low-maintenance border like this is best planted on either side of a hard path, or set with stepping stones for access.

Self-sufficient border

In genuine old cottage gardens, vegetables and flowers intended to be cut for sale were grown in rows in a separate garden at the rear of the house, where the plants could be kept free from

Ground covering perennials, such as hostas, smother out weeds once they have filled out.

competing weeds or pests and spaced out for maximum growth. If the layout of the land made it necessary to place the vegetable patch at the side of the house, it often had a flower border growing along the side to screen it slightly, but other than that vegetables and flowers were not mixed.

However, from Victorian times it became fashionable to grow vegetables with herbs, flowers and fruit in the same bed for romantic effect. Although vegetables would not have done so well in company and are far more at risk from pests, which find plenty of cover in the surrounding thickets of plants, you can certainly pick some usable crops. This is an attractive way of growing plants that evoke the self-sufficient spirit of an old cottage garden.

Good plants to use in vegetable and flower beds include herbs originally intended for household use such as curled tansy (*Tanacetum vulgare* var. *crispum*), medicinal plants, such as comfrey (*Symphytum officinale*), bee plants like lavender, edible flowers, such as borage, flowers for cutting like dahlias, and decorative vegetables such as red-leaved forms of kale or purple-podded peas. You could even include flowers formerly used in folklore, such as St John's wort (*Hypericum tetrapterum*), or witchcraft, such as vervain (*Verbena officinalis*). The result is very picturesque, educational for children, and forms a long-standing conversation piece for visitors to the garden.

COLLECTORS' TREASURES

Choice, old and scarce cottage garden flowers need to be kept entirely separate from the thugs that would soon over-run them. Without enough light and air, small, delicate or slow-growing plants soon succumb to mildews, slug and snail attacks, and other pests, diseases and disorders arising from poor growing conditions.

The aim should be to get to know the individual needs of collectors' plants and give them their ideal conditions, rather than trying to fit them into the general rough-and-tumble of the garden. This might mean preparing a special bed for them, into which other carefully vetted plants are added to vary the effect and extend the flowering season.

Different groups of plants need different conditions.

Old-fashioned primroses and polyanthus, including the gold-laced type, like light dappled shade, with lots of leafmould or coir, well-rotted garden compost and horticultural grit to provide the classic moisture-retentive but well-drained conditions. It is essential to divide the clumps every year or two shortly after flowering to prevent them dying out.

Other old cottage flowers that are close relatives of native wildflowers, such as the double form of red campion (*Silene dioica* 'Flore Pleno'), double lady's smock (*Cardamine pratensis* 'Flore Pleno') and double celandines (*Ranunculus ficaria* cultivars), enjoy similar conditions, but with more sun. These tend to survive without frequent division, but even so it is a good idea to propagate them in order to have replacements in case of losses.

Old varieties of perennial wallflowers, such as *Erysimum cheiri* 'Harpur Crewe' and 'Bloody Warrior', like a fairly sunny, open situation with well-drained, moisture-retentive soil. They are very short-lived perennials, which must be propagated from cuttings every two or three years, as they do not produce seed and old plants become too woody to produce suitable material for cuttings.

Old pinks (*Dianthus*) need poor soil and a very sunny, well-drained situation, so a raised bed is often the most satisfactory way of growing them well.

Pinks are worth growing for their spicy scent alone, though the flowers are also good for cutting. Modern varieties will flower continuously all summer.

Roses contrast well with tall spikes of flowers like these delphiniums.

OLD ROSES

In cottage-style gardens, old roses are not grown in formal rose beds. It is an unwritten rule of cottage gardening that you should never see any bare soil, just a complete carpet of plants. Since most old roses have a short flowering season – in early summer – it makes sense to underplant them with a varied tapestry of spring bulbs and cottage flowers that are in bloom during the rest of the summer, to make the most of the space that is available.

Taller flowers for planting between the roses towards the back of the border include clumps of Madonna lilies (*Lilium candidum*) and light, airy flowers, such as *Thalictrum delavayi* 'Hewitt's Double' or *Verbena bonariensis*. Biennials, such as sweet Williams (*Dianthus*) and Canterbury bells (*Campanula medium*), are also good for growing in between roses. The front of the border and around the feet of rose bushes is the ideal place to grow flowers such as double red campion (*Silene dioica* 'Flore Pleno') and *Campanula persicifolia*, which are notoriously difficult to place anywhere else. Their tall spikes of flower appear from low, wide-spreading mats of foliage, which are easily swamped under taller plants in a typically riotous cottage flower border.

Fans of one particular genera of cottage flowers often like to mass plant their favourites together under roses, as long as they enjoy the same growing conditions. William Robinson, the Victorian gardening writer who led the move towards natural plantings and the use of wild flowers, was in favour of growing carpets of violets under roses, but today hardy cranesbills (*Geranium*) are more commonly collected. A mixture of different types gives a succession of flowers, varied plant shapes and sizes, and attractive foliage – including some autumn colour – from late winter through until mid-autumn the following year.

RAISED BEDS AND CONTAINERS

Raised beds and containers are a good way to pack more plants into a limited space and to soften hard features like porches, paving and gravel. They also make it possible to add height to an otherwise level garden, which helps to show off a large collection of flowers to better effect by lifting some up above the others. In a garden that is made up mainly of closely packed flowers, an occasional element of architecture makes a useful design feature, as it allows you the opportunity to create contrasts. However, from a plant-lover's point of view probably the biggest advantage of containers and raised beds is that they make it possible to grow plants that would not be happy in the garden soil, since it is very easy to buy or mix special composts for particular purposes.

In a garden where the ground is badly drained or consists of heavy clay, containers and raised beds are particularly valuable for growing evergreen herbs, bulbs such as crown imperials (*Fritillaria imperialis*), tulips and lilies, or rock plants, all of which dislike winter wet. They are also good places to grow your treasures, as the plants will be more likely to receive individual attention and avoid being swamped by more vigorous plants.

Although modern containers and walling materials can be used, for a more natural, cottagey effect, old reclaimed items are best. Good containers include clay pots (old ones are sometimes available at nurseries or turn up in junk shops), old chimney pots (from architectural salvage yards) or clay land-drainage pipes stood on end (from agricultural merchants). Old stone troughs or sinks and old household pots and pans can all be used.

In a garden full of flowers, you need an occasional architectural element, such as this bench, for contrast.

Containers look best grouped together around the front and back doors, or in corners on paved and gravelled areas around hardwood seats. Make sure they are out of the way of areas you need to cross with machinery or hosepipes, but where you have easy access for watering, dead-heading and other regular attention.

Raised beds can be made from old bricks or tiles (again, from architectural salvage yards and some builders' merchants), reconstituted stone, which can be bought to resemble dry stone walling, or various types of second-hand timber including railway sleepers and old telegraph poles.

Mark out the site for a raised bed, strip off any existing turf or clear weeds, and excavate the top few centimetres of topsoil. Construct low retaining walls – for flowers, a depth of 45–60cm (1½–2ft) is quite adequate, although you can make the bed

deeper if required. For most cottage flowers, the bed can be filled with good topsoil and a generous addition of well-rotted organic matter.

However, if you intend to grow plants that need very sharp drainage, fill the base with builders' rubble, bricks or broken clay flowerpots to a depth of 10–15cm (4–6in). Place a layer of coarse organic material, such as partially rotted old turves placed upside down, all over the stones, and fill the bed with a mixture of good, weed-free topsoil, coir or leafmould and horticultural grit. For plants that need serious drainage, such as old pinks (*Dianthus*) and rock plants, use up to 25 per cent each by volume of grit and coir or leafmould, but for evergreen herbs and bulbs ten per cent each of coir and grit is plenty.

COTTAGE GARDEN FLOWERS FOR CUTTING

From Victorian times, cottagers grew certain flowers – particularly sweet peas, gladioli and dahlias – in rows in the vegetable garden to sell as cut flowers at the garden gate. Nowadays, flowers for cutting are likely to be grown in normal borders and cut sparingly to avoid spoiling the garden, although more serious flower arrangers may make a special cutting garden for their own use, containing a wide range of favourite cut flowers.

Achillea millefolium
Perennial
Around 60cm (2ft) (depending on cultivar)
Coloured forms of wild yarrow with various named varieties, old and new. Flat heads of red, pink or yellow for most of the summer.

Achillea ptarmica The Pearl Group
Perennial
1m (3ft)
Double form of wild *Achillea ptarmica*, which was once grown as a medicinal plant. Clusters of double white flowers throughout summer.

Aster
Half-hardy annual and perennial
Around 1m (3ft) depending on cultivar
'Ostrich Plume' asters are still great favourites for cutting, but perennial types, such as *Aster ericoides,* × *Solidaster luteus* (a hybrid of *Solidago* and perennial Aster), and New England and Michaelmas daisies (*Aster novae-angliae* and *A. novi-belgii*) are all good for cutting.

Astrantia major
Perennial
30–45cm (12–18in)
Compact plants with shaggy, greenish white, pink or red pincushion flowers and attractive foliage all summer. Self seeds freely.

Chrysanthemum zawadskii
Perennial
around 75cm (2½ft) depending on cultivar
The original cottage chrysanthemums, completely hardy so can be left outside all year. A range of varieties in pink, bronze, mahogany, white and yellow shades, flowering in very late autumn.

Dahlia
Tender tuber
1–2m (3–6ft)
Available in an enormous range of flower colours, sizes and shapes. Plant in late spring, and dig up tubers up in mid-autumn to store in a frost-free place under cover for winter. Traditionally grown in rows in the vegetable patch, to sell as cut flowers by the garden gate.

Gladiolus
Tender corm
1–1.2m (3–4ft)
Traditionally grown in rows in the vegetable garden, for cutting to sell. Plant a few corms every two weeks from early to late spring, for a succession of flowers for cutting through

Dame's violet is a real old-fashioned flower that is useful as a filler in the garden and in a vase.

the summer. Harvest corms in autumn and store in a frost-free place.

Lathyrus odoratus
Hardy annual

2m (6ft)

Any sweet peas qualify as cottage garden flowers, but several old varieties – such as the 18th century red-and-white 'Painted Lady' – are still available. Small flowers by today's standards, but many seed companies supply mixtures of old varieties especially for their strong scent.

COTTAGE GARDEN FLOWERS FOR SCENT

One of the first essentials for a cottage garden is scent. Arrange plants so that you wander from one perfume to another, and plan for a succession of different fragrances throughout the season.

Convallaria majalis
Perennial

20cm (8in)

Originally a British native, lily of the valley produces arching stems of white bells in spring, then dies down in summer.

Dianthus
Evergreen perennial

25–45cm (9–18in)

Old-fashioned pinks often have a strong clove scent, with some varieties more scented than others – consult specialist catalogues.

Hesperis matronalis
Short-lived perennial

75cm (2½ft)

Sweet rocket or dame's violet has very pale pink flowers all summer; *Hesperis matronalis* var. *albiflora* is white. Both self seed. Rare old double forms are occasionally available.

Jasminum officinale
Woody climber
6m (20ft)
Very strongly perfumed white flowers in clusters, all summer.

Lathyrus odoratus
Hardy annual
2m (6ft)
Old fashioned varieties with smaller flowers are the best for scent
– scented mixtures are now sold by most seed firms.

Lavandula × intermedia angustifolia
Small shrubs
60cm–120cm (2–4ft)
Strongly aromatic leaves and fragrant, pale purple flowers in
mid- to late summer. Traditionally dried to make lavender
bags to repel moths from cupboards.

Lilium candidum
Bulb
1m (3ft)
Very old lily, with white flowers. Madonna lily prefers
shallow planting in light, chalky soil without disturbance

Lonicera periclymenum
Woody climber
5m (15ft)
Wild woodbine of hedgerows. Pale cream-and-apricot
flowers in mid- to late summer. Occasionally self seeds
where shed by birds.

Nepeta 'Six Hills Giant'
Perennial
75cm (2½ft)
Rich lemon-scented foliage, much appreciated by cats
(hence 'catmint'), and deep lavender flowers all summer.

Grow catmint close to the edge of a path, as the leaves must be crushed in order to release the scent.

Nicotiana alata
Half-hardy annual
60–120cm (2–4ft)
Old-fashioned tobacco plants were tall, white only and well-scented but only opened in the evening; modern varieties lost their scent but now some are being bred specially for this characteristic, such as *Nicotiana × sanderae* 'Sensation', 'Evening Fragrance' and 'Perfume', with mixed colours and flowers that stay open during the day.

Rosa
Shrubs
1–2.2m (3–7ft) depending on cultivar
Not all old roses are heavily scented, but the best varieties are overwhelming – consult specialist catalogues.

Viola odorata
Perennial
15cm (6in)
Named varieties of sweet violet are collectors' plants, varying from unperfumed to strongly scented. Parma violets have the best scent but must be grown under glass.

Choosing cottage garden flowers

Of the many hundreds – probably thousands – of different cottage flowers available, I only have room to recommend a very limited selection, so I have deliberately chosen the more traditional 'cottage classics'. Nurseries specialising in cottage garden plants will also have many more modern plants that are equally deserving of space.

Alcea rosea

Hollyhock

Hollyhocks at the gate is the hallmark of an old cottage garden, as depicted in Victorian watercolours. The plants have been grown in cottage gardens since the 15th century. Besides the traditional pale pink, cream and mauve shades, there is also a gleaming chocolate-maroon, *Alcea rosea* 'Nigra', and modern strains with brighter colours, including double varieties with powder-puff-like flowers.

Hollyhocks are short-lived perennials, but nowadays, due to ever-present problems with rust, they are normally treated as biennials and pulled out after flowering to eliminate diseased foliage. If they are allowed to self seed, the surviving seedlings tend to show slight natural rust resistance, but unfortunately they usually have very dull, watery-coloured flowers. However, when rust is a real problem and you pine to grow hollyhocks, go for the fig-leaved species *Alcea ficifolia*, which looks very similar but has some rust resistance.

Grow hollyhocks from seed sown where they are to flower in midsummer, or sow in a nursery bed to transplant in

Hollyhocks are the stuff of Victorian watercolours and where rust isn't a problem, they are still real charmers.

autumn. The plants flower in early to midsummer, and the stems are strong enough to stand up without any staking. Hollyhocks will grow in most soil, in sun.

Height: 15–20cm (6–8in)
Spread: 45cm (18in)
Planting distance: 38cm (15in)
Hardiness: H4, USA to zone 7

Alchemilla mollis

Lady's mantle

The true Lady's mantle is actually *Alchemilla xanthochlora* (syn. *A. vulgaris*), which has considerable medicinal properties – the botanical name comes from the Arabic word for alchemy, after its purportedly miraculous properties. The common name is correctly spelt 'Lady's' rather than 'ladies'', since the plant is named after Our Lady.

However, *Alchemilla mollis* has become a popular cottage garden plant in comparatively recent times due to its good gardening qualities. Its dense, compact habit, pleated fan-like leaves, and long-lasting sprays of tiny lime-green flowers in early to midsummer make it invaluable for underplanting a multicoloured cottage garden border for continuity, and to separate potentially clashing colours. The flowers can also be cut and used fresh or dried.

Alchemilla is perennial and prefers well-drained soil in sun or light shade. It self seeds readily into difficult places, such as gravel paths or cracks between paving, creating a pleasingly natural effect. Neat and tidy gardeners often complain about its wandering habits, but in a cottage garden that is often considered to be an asset.

Height: 30cm (12in)
Spread: 30cm (12in)
Planting distance: 20cm (8in)
Hardiness: H4, USA to zone 7

Aquilegia vulgaris
Columbine, granny's bonnets

Another old cottage classic, the long-spurred flowers of aquilegias have been grown in cottage gardens since the 13th century. Modern strains include an enormous range of colours, a few quite compact forms, and some with upward-facing flowers. *Aquilegia* Biedermeier Group is particularly attractive, with almost spurless flowers in the shape of Victorian jelly moulds.

Aquilegias are short-lived perennials that flower from late spring to early summer. They self seed very freely and cross-pollinate indiscriminately, producing huge numbers of enchanting mongrels – unless you curb their activities by dead-heading the plants, or treat them as biennials and pull them up when the flowers are over. However, it is worth leaving self-sown seedlings that come up in suitable places, since they establish themselves without needing to be kept watered, tolerate much worse conditions than pot-grown plants and usually have perfectly good flowers. A minor drawback of self-sown seedlings is that compact strains of parents produce much taller offspring.

Sow aquilegias in late spring or early summer where they are to flower, or sow in trays and prick out the seedlings into pots – they are not keen on root disturbance. They grow well in sun or light shade, in any reasonable soil as long as it holds moisture.

Height: 45–100cm (18–39in) depending on variety
Spread: 20–30cm (8–12in) depending on variety
Planting distance: 20cm (8in)
Hardiness: H4, USA to zone 7

Astrantia

Masterwort, Hattie's pincushion

Astrantias are well known for their extraordinary, spiky-looking, pincushion-shaped flowers that are produced throughout the summer in shades of pale green, white, pink or, in the case of some of the most sought-after newer varieties such as *Astrantia* 'Hadspen Blood', purplish red. *A. major* subsp. *involucrata* 'Shaggy' is particularly well named, with large, loose greenish-white flowers.

Astrantias are compact plants with wonderful foliage. Variegated forms such as *A. major* 'Sunningdale Variegated' tend to revert to plain green in summer, but they can be restored by cutting them back close to the ground – the new growth that soon appears is as good as new.

Astrantias grow best in any moist, reasonably good soil and they prefer light shade although, contrarily, self-sown seedlings turn up freely even in dry, sunny spots. Seed germinates best when it drops fresh from the plant – old seed has very poor germination – so rely on self-sown mongrel seedlings to increase your stock, or buy named varieties in pots and divide them when big enough if you want to keep plants that are true to type.

Height: 30–45cm (12–18in)
Spread: 30cm (12in)
Planting distance: 20cm (8in)
Hardiness: H4, USA to zone 7

Clematis

It may seem a contradiction in terms to list such highly fashionable plants among old-fashioned cottage garden flowers, but the looks and growth habit of clematis suit them perfectly to cottage garden-style growing and they are deservedly popular for this purpose.

The larger kinds, such as named varieties of *Clematis viticella*, like to scramble up through trees and shrubs, then burst out at the top to form a canopy of flowers. *C. viticella* 'Purpurea Plena

Elegans' is a particular favourite, with rosette-shaped, double parma-violet flowers straight from a painting by an Old Master – and it is in fact very old, being mentioned in Parkinson's Herbal of 1629.

Medium-sized clematis are good for growing on pillars in a border or over an arch with climbing roses, and this method particularly suits large-flowered hybrids such as the old pink-and-puce striped *Clematis* 'Nelly Moser'. More compact varieties, such as shell-pink 'Hagley Hybrid', also make very good plants for growing in containers and even large hanging baskets, as long as you choose varieties with a long flowering season and keep them very well fed and watered.

The true clematis species are also much grown by modern cottage gardeners. The compact *Clematis alpina* is a charmer, flowering in early spring with nodding blue lantern flowers; it needs no pruning and is good for growing on a rustic hazel or willow plant support in a border.

Clematis prefer rich, fertile soil and most of them are happy in both sun and light shade, but their ideal situation is one where their roots are in cool shade and their stems in the sun. Feed plants generously in spring, and prune varieties that need it down to 15cm (6in) above ground level in late winter; tidy others lightly at the same time. Overgrown plants, even of varieties that do not normally need pruning, can be cut back hard in late winter to rejuvenate them if needed, although you may miss the following season's flowering.

Height and spread: vary according to species and variety
Planting distance: n/a
Hardiness: H4, USA to zone 7

Cymbalaria muralis
Ivy-leaved toadflax

Although it is always thought of as a British native wildflower, ivy-leaved toad- flax is, in fact, a 17th-century introduction that liked us so much that it ran wild. A compact, trailing plant with small, glossy ivy-shaped leaves and charming lilac-and-yellow flowers, like tiny snapdragons, all summer, it is superb for dry places in sun or light shade. It is especially valuable for its habit of naturalising itself in chinks in brickwork and old walls, even where there is very little soil. Spare seedlings salvaged from around the garden make good plants for tubs and hanging baskets – plant them into the previous year's old compost, as they prefer low levels of nutrients. Stems root as they run along, in time forming modest-sized mats of interconnected plants.

Height: 5cm (2in)
Spread: 30cm (12in)
Planting distance: 10cm (4in)
Hardiness: H4, USA to zone 7

Dianthus
Pink, gillyflower

Modern pinks, such as the ever-reliable and long-flowering *Dianthus* 'Doris', make good cottage garden flowers for a hot, sunny spot with free-draining soil. The old varieties are real collectors' pieces, grown for their heady clove scent and curious laced flowers, like the 18th-century 'Paisley Gem', or clock-face patterned blooms such as 'Sops-in-Wine'. Some varieties, such as 'Fenbows Nutmeg Clove' (which can be traced back to the 17th century or earlier), were once grown outside inns and used to flavour mulled wine, but many old pinks have been lost and found over the centuries so their original names and past history have been mislaid.

Old-fashioned pinks need very light, free-draining, sandy or gritty soil with little or no organic matter and low fertility, so if the garden soil is unsuitable it is advisable to make a raised bed specially for them. The plants are quite short lived and must be propagated every two or three years if you are to avoid losing them. Do this from 'pipings', which are tip cuttings made by tugging out the shoot from a node with a nice knobbly knuckle, just after the flush of summer flower is over. Choose a non-flowered shoot; remove the lower leaves as usual and push each cutting into an individual 8cm (3in) pot containing a 50:50 mix of seed compost and silver sand or fine grit. Keep the cuttings in a shady place until they have rooted, which takes about six to eight weeks in midsummer, and do not put a plastic bag over the top as they tend to rot easily.
(see p.48)

Height: 23–45cm (9–18in) depending on variety
Spread: 23–60cm (9–24in) depending on variety
Planting distance: 23–30cm (9–12in)
Hardiness: H4, USA to zone 7

Dicentra spectabilis
Bleeding heart, lady in the bath
This currently fashionable perennial of 'smart' gardens began life as a cottage garden flower. It boasts elegantly arching sprays of red-and-white, locket-shaped flowers in late spring and early summer, and delicate ferny foliage. Generations of small boys must have picked a flower, turned it upside-down and pulled back the outer petals to reveal the lady sitting in her bath, although this takes a fairly vivid imagination – and ideally the all-white form, *Dicentra spectabilis* 'Alba', in order to see her properly. Nevertheless, dicentra is invaluable for adding spring colour to moist, shady corners where there is plenty of

organic matter, and for growing between shrubs, whose twiggy stems help to support the plants' rather fragile stems. The plant conveniently dies down in midsummer, leaving room for neighbouring plants to spread out. Propagate by seed or division.

Height: 1m (3ft)
Spread: 45cm (18in)
Planting distance: 38cm (15in)
Hardiness: H4, USA to zone 7

Digitalis purpurea
Foxglove

This is a British native with tall, upright spikes of spotty, finger-stall-shaped, mauve summer flowers, much loved by bees. Foxgloves like woodland conditions – moist, humus-rich soil and light, dappled shade. Cultivated forms, such as the popular *Digitalis purpurea* Excelsior Group, come in a wider range of colours; Gloxinioides Group is an old variety with wide-open, forward-facing, frilly-edged spotty flowers of many colours; *D. purpurea* f. *albiflora* has pure white flowers that look almost ghostly among tree trunks at twilight.

Foxgloves are short-lived perennials, often treated as biennials in gardens. Sow seed in trays in early to midsummer, prick out the seedlings into pots and plant them out in their flowering position in autumn. Plants left in the ground self seed readily, producing fascinating mongrels.
(see p.39)

Height: 1–2m (3–6ft) depending on variety
Spread: 45–60cm (1½–2ft) depending on variety
Planting distance: 30–38cm (12–15in)
Hardiness: H4, USA to zone 7

Erysimum cheiri
Wallflower

Wallflowers are wonderful old-fashioned, late-spring-flowering bedding plants with a bewitching warm, spicy scent. They are best for planting in beds on either side of the front door, or in large clay flowerpots, although they are also good for filling odd gaps as they appear around the garden in autumn. They associate stunningly well with tulips.

Bedding wallflowers are treated as biennials, sown in early to midsummer in a vacant row in the vegetable garden, then thinned out to a few centimetres apart and transplanted to their flowering positions in autumn. Various single-colour and mixed strains are available including some quite compact ones, but to my mind the most cottagey-looking is the old *Erysimum cheiri* 'Persian Carpet', a rich mix of cream, red, apricot and gold shades that is still available from a few seed companies.

Wallflowers do well in any reasonably good soil in sun or partial shade. Plants left *in situ* after flowering will often self seed into hot, dry chinks in walls and cracks in paving and stonework, where nothing you planted deliberately would ever survive. These self-sown seedlings are very compact and rugged, usually with small, plain orange or yellow flowers that are nonetheless very pretty.

Perennial wallflowers are found in plant catalogues, including the double *E. cheiri* 'Bloody Warrior'. They are short-lived perennials and must be propagated regularly from cuttings, as they soon become somewhat bare and woody. They like a hot, dryish, sunny spot.

Height: 30–45cm (12–18in)
Spread: 15–20cm (6–8in)
Planting distance: 15cm (6in)
Hardiness: H4, USA to zone 7

Fritillaria imperialis
Crown imperial

Natives of Turkey that reached England around the end of the 16th century, crown imperials feature in Shakespeare's works and were great favourites in formal gardens of the time. They reached cottage gardens around the turn of the 20th century, and black-and-white photographs of the time often show them growing in rows through a carpet of short groundcover plants, along the edge of a path. In spring, the species produces a circle of big, tubular, tawny orange flowers underneath a topknot of foliage, perched on top of an almost mathematically symmetrical plant. Double-flowered forms, red or yellow varieties and some with variegated foliage are also occasionally available. Particularly strange is *Fritillaria imperialis* 'Prolifera' (syn. 'Crown upon Crown'), which has two tiers of flowers, one on top of the other, like an Edwardian cakestand.

Buy dry bulbs in autumn and plant them in fertile, moisture-retentive but well-drained soil enriched with plenty of well-rotted manure, in full sun. If the garden soil is not suitable, grow crown imperials in large pots to plunge into the border and remove them to the safety of a cold frame after flowering. All parts of the plant, but particularly the bulbs, smell strongly of foxes – they have been suggested for growing as a deterrent to rabbits. Propagate from seed, though they are usually bought as dormant bulbs in spring.

Height: 1m (3ft)
Spread: 30cm (12in)
Planting distance: 23cm (9in)
Hardiness: H4, USA to zone 7

Fuchsia 'Riccartonii'

Hardy fuchsia

This exotic-looking shrub resembles a tender fuchsia but has smaller leaves and long, narrow, elegant, dangling red-and-purple flowers like earrings, from the tube of which emerge even longer, straight, whiskery stamens. The plant has an exceptionally long flowering season, from midsummer well into late autumn, right up to the first real frost.

As this fuchsia is not reliably hardy, it is often killed off to ground level in a cold winter, but as long as the crown is protected with a few shovelfuls of leaf litter or similar insulating material, a well-established plant will reshoot in spring in time to flower well again all summer. In mild areas, where plants do not die down, they can form quite tall bushes and are sometimes used as flowering hedges.

Grow hardy fuchsias in a sunny, sheltered spot with well-drained soil. Cuttings root easily throughout the summer.

Height: 1–2m (3–6ft)
Spread: 1–1.2m (3–4ft)
Planting distance: 60cm (2ft)
Hardiness: H3, USA to zone 8/9

Geranium

Hardy cranesbill

A large family of excellent and deservedly fashionable groundcover perennials, hardy cranesbills have a long flowering season and some can also produce good autumn leaf colour. Use scrambling kinds for creeping around the bottom storey of cottage garden borders and planting under old roses; taller types that make independent clumps are good for planting between shrubs or with other herbaceous flowers.

Geranium psilostemon has rather loud magenta flowers and makes a large mound with big, deeply cut leaves. *G. macrorrhizum* makes a lower mound with pink flowers in late spring, and it is one of the earliest species to flower. G. *phaeum* is a taller, more upright species with deep maroon-black flowers, which grows in deeper shade than most. G. *pratense* 'Mrs Kendall Clark' is a very popular upright, clump-forming variety with white-veined, sky blue flowers.

The plants grow in any reasonable soil with some moisture. Propagate them from basal cuttings, or divide established plants. Many cranesbills self seed gently and hybridise, producing interesting new offspring.

Height: 30–60cm (1–2ft)
Spread: 60–100cm (2–3ft)
Planting distance: 60cm (2ft)
Hardiness: H4, USA to zone 7

Helianthus annuus

Sunflower

Sunflowers are old-fashioned hardy annuals with tall, single stems topped by yellow flowers, which were traditionally grown in a row in front of a sunny wall. Now that they have become fashionable there are many more varieties from which to choose, including some with red, orange and mahogany flowers, some shorter, bushier varieties that are good for cutting, and a few very dwarf varieties with double flowers suitable for growing in pots.

Sow sunflower seeds in small pots on the windowsill indoors in early spring, to give them a longer growing season if you want giant varieties to grow to their maximum height; otherwise, sow outside in mid- to late spring where you want the plants to flower. Sunflowers like rich, fertile soil with some moisture, and plenty of sun. Leave the plants in the ground after the flowers are over so that birds can feed on the seeds – if you are planting specifically with birds in mind, they prefer black-seeded varieties to those with large, tough, striped seeds.

Height: 0.6–4m (2–12ft)
Spread: 30cm (12in)
Planting distance: 45cm (18in)
Hardiness: n/a

Hesperis matronalis

Sweet rocket, dame's violet

Sweet rocket is a very old cottage garden flower, known for the haunting evening fragrance of its otherwise not very exciting flowers. The species has a mixture of off-white, pale pink and light mauve flowers; *Hesperis matronalis* var. *albiflora* is pure white, and the rare old double-flowered form 'Lilacina Flore Pleno' is also occasionally available, despite a near-brush with extinction. The plants are short-lived perennials that like a rich, fertile soil. Single varieties self seed gently.

(See p.55)

Height: 75cm (2½ft)
Spread: 30cm (12in)
Planting distance: 30cm (12in)
Hardiness: H4, USA to zone 7

Heuchera

Coral bells

Possibly not authentic old cottage garden plants, heucheras are nevertheless collected by modern cottage gardeners for their attractive leaves, which are often highly coloured, coupled with sprays of airy red, pink or white flowers in early summer. *Heuchera cylindrica* 'Greenfinch' is popular with flower arrangers for its tall, wheat-like heads of green flowers. *H. micrantha* var. *diversifolia* 'Palace Purple' has white flowers set against deep purple leaves,

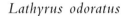

while *H.* 'Pewter Moon' boasts pink flowers and pewter-patterned foliage. Plants retain their leaves reasonably well in all but the worst winters. Propagate by division.

  Height: 30cm (12in)
  Spread: 23cm (9in)
  Planting distance: 23cm (9in)
  Hardiness: H4, USA to zone 7

Lathyrus odoratus

Sweet pea

The first 'sweet pea' in cottage gardens was the everlasting pea, *Lathyrus latifolius*, a perennial, which has been grown around front doors since the 16th century. The hardy annual *L. odoratus* was introduced to this country in 1699 but did not attract much attention, as it looked like a weed with a vanilla-scented purple flower – it took centuries for sweet peas as we know them today to emerge. Many of the earlier varieties were bred by a Shropshire cottage gardener, Henry Eckford, and in 1899 one of his varieties, growing at the Countess Spencer's garden at Althorp, was found to have wavy edges – it was spotted by her gardener, Silas Cole, who developed from it the now-famous Spencer strain of sweet peas.

Sweet peas have been a favourite flower for village shows for about a century, and they were one of the cottage garden staples for growing in rows in the vegetable patch to sell at the garden gate. You still often find bunches of sweet peas on sale outside country cottages, along with eggs and occasional cabbages and marrows. Nowadays, few people other than exhibitors and flower arrangers have the patience to look after cordon-trained sweet peas, but untrained plants are superb for scrambling up netting and ideal for covering the prickly bare lower stems of climbing roses. Modern compact varieties of sweet pea also make good plants for hanging baskets and containers.

Sow sweet pea seeds in early spring in pots under cover and plant out when the weather permits later in spring, or sow in mid-spring where they are to flower. Enthusiasts wanting extra-early flowers for exhibition usually sow the seeds in autumn, but the flowers come to an end in midsummer. Sweet peas need a sheltered, sunny spot with deep, rich, fertile soil. It was once traditional to prepare a special trench for them during the winter, which was filled with rich organic waste, in the same way as for runner beans.

Height: 2m (6ft)
Spread: 30cm (12in)
Planting distance: 15cm (6in)
Hardiness: n/a

Lavandula
Lavender

It is hard to picture a cottage garden without lavender. *Lavandula angustifolia* (syn. *L. spica*) arrived here with the Romans, and was an important medicinal and perfumery plant throughout the Middle Ages. Fifty years ago, lavender flowers were still being gathered in cottage gardens to dry and make into lavender bags to repel clothes moths from bedroom cupboards and chests of drawers. This good habit is due for a comeback, now that natural fibres are back in fashion and moths are up to their old tricks again.

Lavenders were traditionally grown in rows along the edge of a path; compact varieties like *L. angustifolia* 'Vera' can be clipped and used as formal dwarf edgings for herb or knot gardens, but large, strongly scented varieties like the old English lavender we nowadays have to call *L. × intermedia* Old English Group is at its best when allowed to sprawl over paving. The green-flowered *L. viridis* is very different, with a strong balsam-resin scent.

Lavenders need a warm, sunny spot with well-drained soil. Clip them over after flowering has finished in late summer to tidy them up. New plants root easily from cuttings.

Height: 60–100cm (2–3ft) depending on variety
Spread: 60–120cm (2–4ft) depending on variety
Planting distance: 45cm (18in)
Hardiness: most traditional varieties H4, USA to zone 7

Lilium candidum

Madonna lily

The Madonna lily has been grown in this country since the time of the Crusades. It took until Elizabethan times for it to become a popular cottage garden flower, but it has been a firm favourite ever since. The large white flowers, produced in early to midsummer, are strongly perfumed and each trumpet has a conspicuous bunch of yellow anthers in the middle.

Plant the bulbs in spring or autumn as soon as they are available, as they dislike drying out. Choose a sunny position with rich, neutral to slightly chalky soil, where the roots will be shaded by surrounding plants, and plant shallowly, so that the tips of the bulbs are no more than 2.5cm (1in) below ground. Leave clumps to build up until they are seriously overcrowded before splitting them up. Propagate by dividing old clumps.

Height: 1m (3ft)
Spread: 45cm (18in)
Planting distance: 23cm (9in)
Hardiness: H4, USA to zone 7

Lychnis chalcedonica
Jerusalem cross

Like the Madonna lily, this plant is thought to have been brought back from the Crusades and bears flowers made up of masses of small bright red 'crosses' from mid- to late summer. If red seems a difficult colour to fit into a 'traditional' pastel cottage colour scheme, try teaming it with nasturtiums (*Tropaeolum majus*) somewhere out of the way.

Lychnis chalcedonica is ideal for old-fashioned cottage gardens, as it does not need regular lifting and dividing, and grows in any half-way reasonable soil. Cut back plants close to the ground in autumn; propagate by division.

Height: 1m (3ft)
Spread: 60cm (2ft)
Planting distance: 45cm (18in)
Hardiness: H4, USA to zone 7

Matthiola incana
Stock

Scent is an essential ingredient in a cottage garden, and stocks have been old favourites since Elizabethan times – they were once as popular as wallflowers. The famous old East Lothian stocks were discovered in a cottage garden and were sown in spring to flower in autumn, but are not grown much now. The biennial Brompton stocks are widely sold as spring bedding plants as soon as the weather improves enough to plant them out in mid- to late spring; to grow your own, sow the seed in midsummer and either put plants in their flowering positions in autumn or – as is more common nowadays –

keep them in a cold frame or unheated greenhouse and plant out in spring.

Night-scented stock (*Matthiola longipetala* subsp. *bicornis*) is a useful hardy annual for adding perfume anywhere you want it in the garden – almost at the last minute, as plants take only six to eight weeks to flower from seed sown at any time in late spring or summer. They can be sprinkled into containers or beds and borders between other plants and no thinning is required. The flowers are rather pale and unexciting, but modern varieties, such as 'Starlight Scentsation' combine a powerful scent with more colourful bright pastel-pink and mauve shades.

Height: 45cm (18in)
Spread: 15cm (6in)
Planting distance: 10cm (4in)
Hardiness: H4, USA to zone 7

Monarda

Bergamot, Oswego tea

Bergamot is so called because the whole plant is scented like the bergamot orange used to perfume Earl Grey tea. The best-known form, *Monarda* 'Cambridge Scarlet', has flamboyant heads of curved, tubular red flowers radiating outwards daisy-like from a central 'button', from midsummer through to autumn. *M.* 'Croftway Pink' is a soft pink and 'Prärienacht' (syn. 'Prairie Night') is deep violet.

Bergamot is a superb plant for attracting butterflies and bees. It needs a rich, moist soil in sun or light shade. Propagate from basal cuttings or by division.

Height: 75cm (2½ft)
Spread: 60cm (2ft)
Planting distance: 45cm (18in)
Hardiness: H4, USA to zone 7

Narcissus
Daffodil

Cottage gardens and the old orchards often associated with them are traditionally a riot of naturalised daffodils in spring. The first kinds to appear in cottage gardens would have been our native Lent lily (*Narcissus pseudonarcissus*) and Tenby daffodil (*N. obvallaris*), but nowadays virtually any daffodils look the part.

For a traditional effect, choose old varieties like the pheasant's eye narcissus (*N. poeticus* var. *recurvus*), which is very late flowering with a strong scent and good for naturalising. It has large flowers of the traditional narcissus shape, with white petals and a short orange cup in the centre. The old spiky-petalled yellow double daffodil *N.* 'Rip Van Winkle' also has a very traditional cottage garden character. Of the modern cultivars, 'Jetfire' is outstanding as it naturalises well, multiplies readily, and looks like a proper yellow-and-orange trumpet 'daff', but with a slightly dwarf habit and short foliage that does not look untidy after the flowers are over.

Plant daffodil bulbs in autumn. Most reasonable soils that hold some moisture are suitable, in sun or light, dappled shade, including under deciduous trees.

Height: 30–45cm (12–18in) depending on variety
Spread: 15cm (6in)
Planting distance: 8–10cm (3–4in)
Hardiness: H4, USA to zone 7

Nepeta
Catmint

Cottages, cats and catmint are natural partners. *Nepeta cataria* is the one cats are supposed to like best, but its lemon-mint scent is not that attractive to us humans and the small mauve-white flowers are rather unexciting, even though the plant is said to be a very good mosquito repellent. *N. mussinii* is much more ornamental, with mounds of grey-green foliage and lavender flowers freely produced from early summer to late autumn. It is an excellent bee plant. *N.* 'Six Hills Giant' is similar but twice the size and – in my garden at least – is the one that cats always seem to prefer.

Grow catmints in a sunny border with reasonable soil, and propagate by cuttings or division. (See p.57)

    Height: 30–45cm (12–18in)
    Spread: 30–60cm (12–24in)
    Planting distance: 30cm (12in)
    Hardiness: H4, USA to zone 7

Nigella damascena

Love-in-a-mist

A typical multipurpose cottage garden flower, love-in-a-mist is an easily grown hardy annual with flowers something like a cornflower but surrounded by a feathery green 'mist'. *Nigella damascena* 'Miss Jekyll' is an old Edwardian favourite with sky-blue flowers; Persian Jewels Series comes in a mixture of pink, mauve, blue and white.

Nigella can be naturalised in a border by scattering the seeds or planting young plants and allowing them to self seed – which they do, but not enough to become a nuisance. It can also be grown in rows, to be cut in full bloom for fresh flowers or left until the petals fall and the seedpods ripen, surrounded by a mist of twiggy bits, to be dried for winter arrangements. The dry seedheads can also be picked off individually and added to a bowl of pot-pourri. Nigella grows in any reasonable soil, in sun or light shade.

    Height: 1m (3ft)
    Spread: 20cm (8in)
    Planting distance: 15cm (6in)
    Hardiness: n/a

Pelargonium

Pelargoniums are old favourites for growing indoors on a cottage windowsill, or outside in the summer in battered clay pots around the door. They have only been cottage flowers since Victorian or Edwardian times. Being frost tender, it is doubtful if many would have made it through the winter on a windowsill in the days before central heating. They would have been dried off and kept in a store room

Many old named varieties that grow naturally leggy somehow look the part better than neat and tidy, bushy modern bedding varieties, and a surprising number of these are still available from specialist nurseries. Old red pelargoniums like single *Pelargonium* 'Paul Crampel' and semi-double 'Gustav Emich' are very traditional, but salmon shades such as 'Mrs Cannell', another very old variety, are often more to modern tastes.

Grow pelargoniums in clay pots of John Innes No. 2 and avoid feeding them until late summer, otherwise the plants will grow leaves at the expense of flowers. Propagate new plants from cuttings in late summer; keep rooted cuttings frost free in winter and pot up in spring. Do not put pelargoniums outside until late spring, when all risk of frost has passed.

(See p.35)

Height: 38cm (15in)
Spread: 20cm (8in)
Planting distance: 15cm (6in)
Hardiness: H1, USA to zone 10/11

Polygonatum multiflorum
Solomon's seal

A long-lived woodland perennial, Solomon's seal was once used for healing purposes, but it makes a good garden plant for late-spring and early-summer interest in shady areas. The fat buds push up through the soil and slowly develop into thick, arching stems dotted with pairs of oval leaves and rows of dangling, greenish-white bell flowers that associate wonderfully with late spring bulbs and primroses. The variegated *Polygonatum* × *hybridum* 'Striatum' is much more spectacular-looking, with neat, cream-striped leaves. The less common *P. odoratum* is similar but

smaller, and worth looking out for as the flowers are scented of tuberoses. All need moist, fertile, humus-rich soil and light shade. Propagate by division.

Height: 75cm (2½ft)
Spread: 30cm (12in)
Planting distance: 20cm (8in)
Hardiness: H4, USA to zone 7

Primula

Primrose and polyanthus

Wild primroses (*Primula vulgaris*) are still grown in damp, shady grass in some cottage gardens today, but unusual, old named varieties are collected by enthusiasts. Some of the strangest are the 'hose-in-hose' type, which look as if one flower has been tucked inside another, and 'Jack-in-the-greens', which have large, frilly green sepals surrounding the flowers like Elizabethan ruffs. Both types are still available from a few specialist nurseries. Give them all standard primrose conditions – a moist, humus-rich border in light shade.

Old polyanthus need a slightly more open, sunny situation with well-drained but moisture-retentive soil and, again, plenty of humus.

Primula 'Guinevere' is one of the easiest to keep, and very pretty with maroonish leaves and primrose-like pink and yellow flowers. Gold-laced polyanthus have small, cowslip-shaped heads of chocolate-maroon flowers edged in gold, creating a delicate, lacy look. These were once old florists' flowers, but have been rescued from the brink of extinction and can now be propagated from seed.

Named varieties of old primroses and polyanthus must be propagated by division, and it is as well to divide the plants every year or two shortly after flowering, otherwise they tend to die out quickly.

Height: 15cm (6in)
Spread: 15cm (6in)
Planting distance: 15cm (6in)
Hardiness: H4, USA to zone 7

Primula auricula

Auricula

Rather cabbage-like evergreen plants with thick, waxy leaves, auriculas have fragrant flowers in late spring and early summer. The old favourite, *Primula auricula* 'Dusty Miller', has floury foliage with red, blue or yellow flowers. Border auriculas can be grown in the garden in a sunny spot with well-drained, fertile but moisture-retentive soil, and allowed to form fair-sized clumps before dividing.

Show auriculas are collectors' plants, some with extraordinary green- or grey-edged flowers marked with 'bullseye' patterns that hardly look real, and were first grown by artisan 'florists' in the 17th century. Nowadays they are grown in pots in a cool, shady cold frame when not in flower, to prevent the powdery 'farina' on the leaves and flowers from being marked by rain, and then brought out when at their peak to exhibit at shows or put on a porch windowsill or shelves in the garden. These plants are divided every year after flowering, so that each pot holds a single specimen with a perfect symmetrical shape.

Height: 20cm (8in)
Spread: 20cm (8in)
Planting distance: 20cm (8in)
Hardiness: H4, USA to zone 7

Pulmonaria

Lungwort

The common name is taken from the Doctrine of Signatures, an old belief that the medicinal properties of certain plants were indicated by the appearance of the plants themselves. In the case of pulmonaria, the spots on the leaves were thought to show that it was intended for treating lung conditions. Nowadays, the plants are grown as good perennial groundcover for their nodding, bell-shaped spring flowers and (usually) spotty foliage in shade; they are also good bee plants.

Pulmonaria rubra 'Redstart' is one of the earliest cottage flowers to bloom in late winter, making a low mound of plain green leaves with terracotta-pink flowers. *P.* 'Sissinghurst White' is particularly elegant, with white flowers and white-spotted leaves. *P. saccharata* Argentea Group has shining silver-white leaves with reddish-violet flowers. Propagate by division.

Height: 30cm (12in)
Spread: 30cm (12in)
Planting distance: 30cm (12in)
Hardiness: H4, USA to zone 7

Rosa

Rose

Old roses are the flowering shrubs of choice in today's cottage gardens, and even though the flowering season is usually limited to roughly six weeks in early summer, they are great characters. Strongly perfumed red rose petals, such as those of the old velvet moss rose *Rosa* 'William Lobb', are good for making into an old delicacy, rose petal

jelly, or for use in pot-pourri. *R. × centifolia* is the old cabbage rose, grown since the Middle Ages, with grey foliage and strongly scented pink flowers reputed to have a hundred petals; it was a great favourite with the old Dutch Master flower painters. *R. × centifolia* 'Cristata' (also known as 'Chapeau de Napoleon') has extraordinary silver-pink flowers with 'moss' forming the shape of a cocked hat on the buds. Rosa Mundi (*R. gallica* 'Versicolor') dates back to the 12th century and was named after Henry II's mistress – 'she' has striped pink, white and crimson flowers on a compact bush, but no scent to speak of. *R.* 'Souvenir de la Malmaison' has fully double, open 'quartered' flowers of the very palest pink and a good scent, but, as with quite a few old roses, the flowers do not last in a cold, wet summer.

Plant old roses in any reasonable, fertile soil in a sheltered, sunny situation and prune to tidy up after flowering – do not prune hard as you would modern bush roses. Large, lax varieties need a framework of rustic poles for support.

Height and spread: 1–2.2m (3–7ft) or more,
    depending on variety
Planting distance: about two-thirds
    of ultimate spread
Hardiness: H4, USA to zone 7

Rosmarinus officinalis
Rosemary

An evergreen shrub used in Tudor times as topiary and for training against walls, rosemary was also traditionally used at weddings and funerals, and had medicinal properties. Gold-variegated rosemary was known as 'gilded rosemary' by Parkinson (the apothecary to James I) and is still available as *Rosmarinus officinalis* 'Aureus'; today, there is also a silver-variegated rosemary named 'Silver Spires'.

Rosemary is good for containers. The Victorians grew the balsam-scented prostrate rosemary (*R. officinalis* Prostratus Group, syn *R. lavandulaceus*) in hanging baskets, but bushy varieties are mainly grown as flowering shrubs that double for cooking purposes. *R. officinalis* 'Severn Sea' has particularly good crops of bright blue flowers; 'Miss Jessopp's Upright' is a tall, upright form with very fine, needle-like leaves, good for hedging.

Grow rosemary in a warm, sheltered spot and very well-drained soil – the plants do not stand winter wet. Propagate from cuttings in summer.

Height: 1m (3ft) depending on variety
Spread: 1.2m (4ft) depending on variety
Planting distance: 1m (3ft)
Hardiness: H4, USA to zone 7

Sedum

Stonecrop

Biting stonecrop (*Sedum acre*) and reflexed stonecrop (*S. rupestre*, syn. *S. reflexum*) are small, low, spreading succulent British natives that appear in dry stone walls and on old roofs, growing in minute deposits of organic matter. They are good for planting in chimney pots, old sinks and big broken terracotta pots laid on their sides in a patch of gravel, as they stand any amount of drought and neglect. Plants are easy to propagate from cuttings or even loose leaves, which quickly take root.

The ice plant (*S. spectabile*) makes a superb butterfly and bee plant, even if it does not have a long history in cottage gardens, as it looks the part and associates well with plants like lavender and catmint in hot, sunny, well-drained borders. The flowers open in late summer and autumn, but the flat green heads of buds add interest for months beforehand. 'Autumn Joy' is a particularly late-flowering form with rusty pink flowers. Propagate by basal cuttings and division.

Height: Sedum spectabile 60cm (2ft)
Spread: Sedum spectabile 30cm (12in)
Planting distance: 30cm (12in)
Hardiness: H4, USA to zone 7

Sempervivum
Houseleek

Clump-forming, small, spiky rosette-shaped succulent plants, houseleeks were traditionally grown on cottage roofs to protect against lightning strike. The cobwebbed houseleek (*Sempervivum arachnoideum*) makes a mat of small, light green rosettes joined together by silky 'webs'. Various named varieties are available with purple, red or grey rosettes. In summer, mature rosettes produce a fat spire topped with pink flowers from the centre.

Houseleeks are good plants for gravelled areas, pots, troughs and even hanging baskets, and they associate well with stonecrops. They need a hot, sunny spot and poor, very well-drained soil. Propagate by detaching offsets in spring or summer.

Height: 5cm (2in)
Spread: 30cm (12in) or more
Planting distance: 15cm (6in)
Hardiness: H4, USA to zone 7

Tropaeolum majus
Nasturtium

Nasturtiums are typical of the 'cheap and cheerful' hardy annuals popular in cottage gardens. It is said that the big orange trumpet flowers are edible and the fresh green seeds reputedly can be pickled as a 'poor man's capers', but there are many better things to eat. Trailing nasturtiums are good for covering a bank and look pretty when allowed to sprawl over a gravel path, as in Monet's garden at Giverny. Compact dwarf varieties are very good for hanging baskets and other containers. *Tropaeolum majus* 'Empress of India' has dark purple-tinged leaves with brilliant scarlet-red flowers, which makes a stunning combination in pots.

Nasturtiums need soil that is low in nutrients, otherwise they produce enormous leaves but no flowers, so grow in a sunny place with rather poor soil. If you are growing them in containers, use seed compost instead of potting compost, or reuse the previous year's old compost. Scatter the seeds in spring where you want the plants to flower, or start them in small pots of seed compost, do not feed them, and plant out the seedlings in late spring when they fill the pots with roots.

Height: 20cm (8in)
Spread: compact varieties 20cm (8in), trailing varieties 1.2m (4ft)
Planting distance: 20cm (8in)
Hardiness: n/a

Viola
Pansy, viola

These small annual, biennial or short-lived perennial flowers are old favourites, grown for their cheerful, round flowers, which often have face-like patterns. Bedding varieties are readily available in garden centres for winter, spring and summer colour, and specialist nurseries list a large range of named old varieties. These include the black-flowered *Viola* 'Molly Sanderson', the unusual gold-and-khaki 'Irish Molly' and the cheeky gold-and-maroon 'Jackanapes', named after Gertrude Jekyll's pet monkey.

Grow violas and pansies (*V.* x *wittrockiana*) in fertile, well-drained but moisture-retentive soil in sun or light shade.

Propagate named varieties from cuttings; sow seed of bedding types in spring or summer, depending on flowering time. They all self seed prolifically and hybridise easily, so self-sown seedlings come up as a fascinating selection of mongrels.

Height: 15cm (6in)
Spread: 20cm (8in)
Planting distance: 20cm (8in)
Hardiness: H4, USA to zone 7

FURTHER INFORMATION

VINTAGE COTTAGE GARDEN FLOWERS TO MATCH OLD HOUSES

Some people who own old cottages like to grow flowers appropriate to the period of their house, and researching the plants that would have been available to Elizabethan, Victorian or Edwardian gardeners is part of the fun. Some nurseries specialising in cottage garden flowers give dates of introduction and other interesting historical facts in their catalogues, and large gardening encyclopedias often list dates. In addition, there are various books specifically on the topic of gardens from different periods in history that can be found in new or second hand bookshops, or borrowed by RHS members from the Lindley Library.

BOOKS

Fish, Margery *Cottage Garden Flowers* (Collingridge, 1961)
Genders, Roy *The Cottage Garden and the Old Fashioned Flowers* (Pelham Books, 1969 and 1983)
Genders, Roy *Growing Old Fashioned Flowers* (David & Charles, 1975)
Sitwell, Sacheverall *Old Fashioned Flowers* (Curwen Press, 1939)
Stewart, David, and Sutherland, James *Plants from the Past* (Penguin Books, 1989)
The Cottage Gardener's Companion (Available from the Cottage Garden Society, see page 90)

The essence of a cottage garden is its flowers, lawns are traditionally absent as they take up valuable space that could be used for the main attraction.

SOCIETIES

Cottage Garden Society, The Administrator, Clive Lane, 'Brandon', Ravenshall, Betley, Cheshire CW3 9BH; tel. 01270 820940; **www.theCGS.org.uk**
National Council for the Conservation of Plants and Gardens (NCCPG), The Stable Courtyard, Wisley Gardens, Woking, Surrey GU23 6Q; **www.NCCPG.org.uk**
Hardy Plant Society, Anne Small, 'Denbeigh', All Saints Road, Creeting St. Mary, Ipswich IP6 8PJ; tel. 01449 711220; **www.hardy-plant.org.uk**

GARDENS TO VISIT

Alfriston Clergy House, The Tye, Alfriston, nr Polegate, East Sussex BN26 5TL; tel. 01323 870001
Anne Hathaway's Cottage, Stratford-upon-Avon; tel. 01789 204016; www.shakespeare.org.uk
East Lambrook Manor, East Lambrook, South Petherton, Somerset TA13 5HL; tel. 01460 240328; **www.eastlambrook.com** (Margery Fish's old garden)

The Cottage Garden Society arranges occasional members' garden open days – details in *The Cottage Gardener* magazine, sent free to members.

Cottage gardens that are open under the National Gardens Scheme can be found by visiting the NGS website (**www.ngs.org.uk**) and searching for cottage gardens.

SUPPLIERS

Bernwode Plants, Kingswood Lane, Ludgershall, Aylesbury, Buckinghamshire HP18 9RB; tel. 01844 237415, **www.bernwodeplants.co.uk**
Cotswold Garden Flowers, Sands Lane, Badsley, Evesham, Worcestershire WR11 5EZ; tel. 01386 42282; **www.cgf.net**
Fibrex Nurseries Ltd, Honeybourne Road, Pebworth, nr Stratford-on-Avon, Warwickshire CV37 8XP; tel. 01789 720799; **www.fibrex.co.uk** (old pelargoniums)
Hardy's Cottage Garden Plants, Freefolk Priors, Freefolk, Whitchurch, Hampshire RG28 7NJ; tel. 01256 896533; **www.hardys-plants.co.uk**

Harvey's Garden Plants, Mulberry Cottage, Bradfield
St George, Bury St Edmunds, Suffolk IP30 0AY;
tel. 01284 386777; **www.harveysgardenplants.co.uk**
Hopley's Plants Ltd, High Street, Much Haddenham,
Hertfordshire SG10 6BU; tel. 01279 842509; **www.hopleys.co.uk**
Langthorn's Plantery, High Cross Lane West, Little Canfield,
Dunmow, Essex CM6 1TD; tel. 01371 872611
Peter Beales Roses, London Road, Attleborough, Norfolk
NR17 1AY; tel. 01953 454707; **www.classicroses.co.uk**

See also the *RHS Plant Finder* for suppliers of particular plants,
and advertisements in *The Cottage Gardener Magazine* magazine.

**The Publisher would like to thank the following people
for their kind permission to reproduce their photographs:**

John Glover: cover image and pages 2, 45, 52 and 89
Harpur Garden Library: pages 7, 13, 15, 21, 23, 29 and 42
© Jerry Harpur; pages 30 and 51 © Marcus Harpur
Clay Perry: pages 1, 8, 11, 19, 33, 40, 46, 48, 49, 80 (bottom)
and 85
Garden Picture Library: p.16 © Mayer/Le Scanff; p. 35 © Jane
Legate; p.39 © Christopher Gallagher; p.39 © Jerry Pavia; p.55
© Pernilla Bergdahl; p.59 © David Cavagnaro; p.60 © Clive
Nichols; p. 61 © Howard Rice; p. 62 and 63 © John Glover;
p.64 © Rowan Isaac; p. 65 © Eric Crichton; p.67 and 68 ©
Howard Rice; p. 69 © Sunniva Harte; p. 70 © JS Sira; p. 72 (top)
© Brian Carter; p.72 (bottom) © Jacqui Hurst; p. 73 © Neil
Holmes; p.74 © Ron Evans; p. 75 (top) © Mark Bolton; p.75
(bottom) © Linda Burgess; p. 76 © Jerry Pavia; p. 78 © John
Glover; p. 80 (top) © Rex Butcher; p.82 (top) © Mayer/Le
Scanff; p.82 (bottom) © David Askham; p.84 (bottom) © Eric
Crichton; p.87 © Howard Rice

INDEX

Page numbers in **bold** refer
to illustrations

Index compiled by
Indexing Specialists (UK) Ltd